ACC Library
DISCARDED
640 Bay Road
Queensbury, NY 12804

P9-APR-267

Filling the Ark

In the series *Animals and Ethics*
Edited by Marc Bekoff

Also in the series
Marc Bekoff, *Animals at Play*

Filling the Ark

Animal Welfare in Disasters

Leslie Irvine

TEMPLE UNIVERSITY PRESS
Philadelphia

Leslie Irvine is Associate Professor of Sociology, University of Colorado at Boulder, and the author of two previous books, including *If You Tame Me: Understanding Our Connection with Animals* (Temple University Press).

Temple University Press
1601 North Broad Street
Philadelphia PA 19122
www.temple.edu/tempress

Copyright © 2009 by Temple University
All rights reserved
Published 2009
Printed in the United States of America

∞ The paper used in this publication meets the requirements of the American National Standard for Information Sciences—Permanence of Paper for Printed Library Materials, ANSI Z39.48-1992

Library of Congress Cataloging-in-Publication Data

Irvine, Leslie.
 Filling the ark : animal welfare in disasters / Leslie Irvine.
    p.   cm. — (Animals and ethics)
  Includes bibliographical references and index.
  ISBN 978-1-59213-834-0 (cloth : alk. paper)
1. Animal welfare—United States. 2. Animal rescue—United States. 3. Disaster relief—United States. 4. Hurricane Katrina, 2005. I. Title.
HV4708.I78 2009
179'.3—dc22

                                                    2008047845

2 4 6 8 9 7 5 3 1

Contents

Acknowledgments

Although my name appears on the cover of this book, I could not have written it without help from numerous people and several institutions. Some of these people shared their knowledge and experience of disasters, some covered my classes while I visited hurricane-stricken regions, some traveled with me to those regions, and others read all or parts of the book in early stages. I would like to thank Jonathan Balcombe, Jenny Bennett, Theo Capaldi, Bridgette Chesne, Susie Coston, Kevin Dennison, Ron Desnoyers, Debra Parsons Drake, Lynelle Dupepe, Ali Hatch, Hal Herzog, Keith Larson, Sean Angus MacKinnon, Sally Matluck, John Pippin, Trish Ritterbusch, Brad Shear, and Kim Sturla. I thank the Department of Sociology and the Natural Hazards Research Center of the University of Colorado, the Humane Society of Boulder Valley, and the Society of Animal Welfare Administrators. I also thank Marc Bekoff, who championed this book throughout the process, and Janet Francendese, of Temple University Press, who provided valuable editorial guidance and support. Finally, the words *thank you* cannot convey the deep appreciation and gratitude I owe my husband, Marc Krulewitch.

Filling the Ark

Introduction

> And of every living thing of all flesh, you shall bring two
> of every kind into the ark, to keep them alive with you;
> they shall be male and female. Of the birds after their
> kind, and of the animals after their kinds, of every creep-
> ing thing of the ground after its kind, two or every kind
> shall come to you to keep them alive.
>
> GENESIS 6:19–20

When a disaster strikes, who should enter the ark? It is widely understood that human lives have priority. But our lives are intertwined with those of billions of non-human animals. Is there a place in the ark for them? If so, which animals should we save? We have the closest relationships with those who are companions, or "pets."[1] We would surely make room on the ark for them. Many people cannot imagine going a day without eating animal products of some sort, and many make a living by raising the animals who provide these products. Clearly, then, we will have to make room for cows, pigs, sheep, chickens, and turkeys. Every prescription medication and most medical procedures are tested on animals before being used on people. The ark will have to accommodate the dogs, cats, primates, rabbits, mice, rats, and guinea pigs used in research. Many zoos in the United States saw record attendance in recent years. Because people enjoy looking at animals, the ark will have to house countless species from all over the world. The ark is becoming crowded, and we have barely scratched the surface of our connections with animals. From the bristles of make-up brushes to the gelatin that encases vitamin supplements, animals are part of our daily routines. As I tell the students who take my course Animals and Society, we like to think of society as distinctly human, with animals existing "on the side," or somehow in their own world. In reality, it is difficult to imagine society without animals. Thus, any event that affects people is likely to affect animals, too. When disasters strike, people are not the only ones who lose lives and homes. We are not the only victims.

This book examines how we make decisions about the treatment of animals in disasters. It encompasses questions about how we determine the worth of animals' lives and how we make distinctions among categories of animals. For example, recent legislation, known as the PETS Act (discussed in Chapter 1), requires states to include companion and service animals in their disaster response plans. Although the enactment of this requirement is a positive step for dogs, cats, and the people who care for them, it highlights the value we place on certain kinds of animals. We humans have determined that dogs and cats can enter the ark. While we applaud ourselves for considering this minority of animals who share our households, the majority of animals who play other roles remain invisible to us. These include animals confined on factory farms, who also suffer and regularly die in disasters. Even the U.S. Department of Agriculture, which regulates agriculture, has no funding or mandate to rescue animals raised for food.

Following Hurricane Katrina, thousands of volunteers converged in Louisiana and Mississippi to assist with the rescue and shelter of companion animals. The effort was a disaster-upon-a-disaster, as animal welfare groups struggled to find ways to feed, house, and care for the endless stream of dogs and cats brought out of stricken areas. Yet, as rescuers roamed the streets of New Orleans, breaking into homes to rescue dogs, cats, birds, and other companion animals, millions of farm animals died because of Katrina. Most were chickens. Those who did not starve or die of thirst and exposure were bulldozed alive into dumpsters. Over eight million birds died in just one producer's facility. The media reports these, and the deaths of other animals used for food, as "losses" for the producers. Their lives are not noted. As Miyun Park of the Humane Society of the United States quotes a typical press report: "According to the American Farm Bureau Federation, farmers in southwestern Louisiana were hurt most by Hurricane Rita, which has resulted in the loss of 30,000 cattle and seriously harmed rice fields and the harvest of sugar cane," adding, "the farmers were hurt, but the cattle were merely 'lost.' Serious harm was reserved for the rice fields."[2]

Whereas most people knew of the plight of companion animals following Katrina, the animals used for food, commonly called "livestock," rarely merited mention. Animals used in research received even less attention. In the downtown New Orleans laboratories of Louisiana State University's Health Sciences Center, eight thousand animals used in research died because of Katrina. Poor planning and no regulations meant that most of the animals drowned in their cages or died of suffocation, starvation, and dehydration.[3] With no chance of escape, those who had not died by a week after the storm were euthanized. What news coverage there was of the Health Sciences Center focused not on the loss of animals' lives but on the loss of valuable "data."

Vulnerability and Species

As the news from the Gulf Region circulated in August and September 2005, it became clear that some human residents suffered significantly more than others did. Some people were able to leave before the flooding began. The world watched as those who remained, particularly the poor, waited for days on rooftops and highway overpasses for help, which for some never came. The captions to photographs showing New Orleans residents carrying water and other supplies described the residents as "looters" or "shoppers," depending on the color of their subjects' skin.[4] Elderly people died in their wheelchairs, lucky to have identification signs hung around their necks. As conditions deteriorated at the Superdome and the Convention Center, the city's shelters of last resort, accusations of racism raged loud. Many residents claimed that if the majority of those unable to evacuate had been white, help would surely have arrived sooner.[5]

Although claims that racism influenced the response and recovery efforts might have been newsworthy for the public, they were by no means news to social scientists engaged in disaster research. For several decades, researchers have examined how various populations experience differential vulnerability to disasters. In what is known as the *vulnerability paradigm*, researchers have argued that disasters are "human-induced, socially constructed events, that is, the hazard itself—the hurricane, the flood, the attack—does not cause the disaster."[6] Rather, the disaster results in the coupling of the hazard with other factors, such as the physical setting, including the built environment, and the capacity of the population to avoid, respond to, and cope with the effects of the incident.[7] Piers Blaikie et al. give the following definition for *vulnerability*:

> The characteristics of a person or group in terms of their capacity to anticipate, cope with, resist, and recover from the impact of a natural hazard. It involves a combination of factors that determine the degree to which someone's life and livelihood is put at risk by a discrete and identifiable event in nature or in society.[8]

In short, the vulnerability of people and groups creates disastrous consequences. The hazard sets off a social process, the outcome of which varies widely. The vulnerability approach highlights the need to look beyond "disasters as simply physical events and consider the social and economic factors that make people and their living conditions unsafe or insecure to begin with."[9] Unlike the blame-the-victim paradigm, the vulnerability paradigm focuses on how the lack of social power makes people unable to influence where and how they live and deprives them of a political voice.

The vulnerability paradigm has produced numerous studies of how pre-existing social inequalities shape disaster impact, response, and recovery. Although a comprehensive review of the literature is beyond the scope of this book, I offer two examples of works that focus on how disasters reflect the organization of a society or a community. *Hurricane Andrew*, an edited volume, examines how the social ecology of Dade County in South Florida meant that residents were differentially affected by that event in 1992.[10] A research team assembled by Walter Peacock provides convincing evidence that race, class, age, gender, and ethnicity matter in disasters. Blocked out of home financing because of the inability to obtain homeowners' insurance, Dade County's disadvantaged minorities often lived in poor quality housing, which was more susceptible to damage. Many minority householders who did have homeowners insurance had insufficient coverage or lacked the supplemental options that would cover temporary housing. After the hurricane, women juggled the tasks of dealing with relief organizations and caring for children and elderly relatives, all while coping with the crowding and lack of privacy in "tent cities" and emergency trailer parks.[11] The increase in divorce and domestic violence following Hurricane Andrew told a story that never made the nightly news.

In *Heat Wave*, Eric Klinenberg accounts for why the heat-related deaths of over seven hundred people in Chicago during the summer of 1995 were not randomly scattered but occurred in particular pockets of the city. Although the official reports describe the heat wave as "a unique meteorological event," Klinenberg portrays it is as an "environmentally stimulated but socially organized catastrophe."[12] By comparing two neighborhoods, one primarily African American and ridden with crime and one Latino, Klinenberg reveals the connections between social factors and heat-related deaths. Elderly African Americans, particularly those living alone, were disproportionately vulnerable to the effects of extreme heat. Their fear of crime and the lack of commercial and community life in the neighborhood forced them to stay home, often with the windows closed. Without social ties to neighbors, they lived—and died—in isolation and in large numbers. Meanwhile, the urban ecology of the contiguous Latino neighborhood made its residents far less vulnerable. Strong social ties, an active Roman Catholic Church, relatively safe streets, and other amenities brought people out of their homes and into contact with one another.

In sum, the vulnerability paradigm avoids treating disasters simply as extreme events and instead directs attention to the social mechanisms that create unequal risks. Studies show how factors including race, class, gender, and ethnicity structure people's options and choices. This book adds species to the list of factors that increase vulnerability. Like us, nonhuman animals have different abilities to cope with and escape hazards. With the exception of wild animals, most have no control over their living conditions. To be sure, different types of animals are vulnerable in different ways. Vulnerability is a variable characteristic, rather than a generalized or intrinsic one. To assert that animals are vulnerable, one must ask which animals are vulnerable, to what, and how.

Among human populations, those most vulnerable to disasters are "those with the fewest choices."[13] As the vulnerability literature has established, the poor, minorities, women, and the elderly often face institutionalized practices of domination and marginalization that limit the choices they can make when faced with natural or technological hazards. By extending this analytical framework to animals, I focus on how different categories of animals are differentially exposed to hazards and are differentially provided opportunities for rescue or escape. For example, although companion animals are vulnerable to abandonment following disasters, they are less vulnerable than animals raised in industrialized farms. Animals such as pigs and chickens, who are locked into cages and dependent on automated systems for food, water, and ventilation, are placed at great risk to numerous hazards and have no chance for escape. Because animals' vulnerability varies by the ways humans have categorized them, it makes little sense to talk about "animals" in disaster, as if they all face the same risk. The discussion must begin by specifying the systematic differences in exposure and protection among different groups or types of animals.

The Sociozoologic Scale

Animals can have many different meanings. As Arnold Arluke and Clinton Sanders put it, "'Being' and animal in modern societies may be less a matter of biology than it is an issue of human culture and consciousness."[14] Whereas some animals are beloved family members, others are pests or vermin. We consider some animals "wild," and whether we kill and eat them depends on the meaning they have for us. People who hunt for meat do not consider dairy cows fair game.[15] Animals have different meanings largely because we categorize them along a hierarchy of worth that Arluke and Sanders call the "sociozoologic scale." Since Aristotle developed the *scala naturae,* we have ranked animals below human beings. Although Darwin and others after him challenged systems that place humans above all other creatures, the idea of a hierarchy remains powerful.[16] Thus, we make distinctions among animals as well as between humans and animals. As Arluke and Sanders argue, scientific challenges to any version of a biological hierarchy will gain little traction because people continue to rank animals along a sociological hierarchy. They explain:

> The desire continues to put animals on some sort of ladder, not because people are ignorant about science—although they certainly might be—but because some dominant ideas linger over many centuries. The history of ideas has demonstrated that certain notions become so pervasive and central to the thought of a culture that over time people uncritically apply these ideas anew.[17]

The sociozoologic system ranks animals in a structure of meaning that allows humans to define, reinforce, and justify their interactions with other beings. We grant some animals a nearly human status, as long as they comply with the code of conduct we establish for them. For example, we give domestic dogs and cats the status of "pets," "companion animals," or family members. However, if they do not comply with the rules, if they exhibit aggression or fear at a level we deem inappropriate, we destroy them because they cannot "fit" into human society. Likewise, other animals who violate the code by their very natures are ignored, despised, or killed. We admire a bear or mountain lion as "wildlife," as long as he or she remains at a distance. Once the animal oversteps the boundaries of the position we have allotted him or her and intrudes into human social space, the "good" creature quickly becomes a dangerous predator who must be eliminated.[18]

Each of the chapters of this book examines a sociozoologic "category" of animals in the context of one or more disaster case studies. For example, hurricanes have posed the most recent and most catastrophic incident to affect companion animals, who occupy a high status on the sociozoologic scale—most of the time. Chapter 1 focuses on Katrina but includes material on Hurricane Andrew, which marked a turning point for the rescue of dogs and cats. Chapter 2 examines the risks faced by the most vulnerable of farmed animals: the chickens who provide meat and eggs. Using two disasters as examples, the chapter shows how different groups of people attribute different value to the lives of chickens and make very different claims about their welfare. In both instances, the factory farming system, not the weather alone, created disastrous consequences. Chapter 3 discusses how oil spills in general affect birds and marine mammals and how specific spills have influenced the rehabilitation of these species. Chapter 4 examines how the location of research facilities can endanger the animals confined within them.

Although in this book I make recommendations for disaster planning and policy, my ambitions are bigger. I make the case for rethinking our use of animals. Consistent with the vulnerability approach, I shed light on our role in putting animals at risk and suggest ways to create more secure conditions. In some instances, "more secure conditions" may mean dramatically changing or ending the use of animals to which we humans have long felt entitled. Also, humans can benefit from reducing the risk to animals. Factory farming provides the best example.

In September 1999, Hurricane Floyd followed closely behind Hurricane Dennis. Together, the storms caused widespread flooding in eastern North Carolina that killed nearly three million animals. Many of these were companion animals, but the great majority were hogs.[19] North Carolina is a major hog-producing state, and most of the animals were housed in concentrated animal feeding operations (CAFOs) on corporate mega-farms. CAFOs for hogs comprise rows of long, low barns or sheds, each of which houses twelve hundred to twenty-five hundred animals. CAFOs use various methods for dealing with manure, but in hog facilities, the animals' waste falls through slots in the floors of the sheds into gutters or pits that are four to ten feet deep. These operations frequently store between three and twelve months' worth of manure beneath the floors.[20] When Hurricane Floyd struck, an estimated 237 hog CAFOs were located on floodplains of eastern North Carolina. Following the hurricane, tens of thousands of hogs drowned in CAFOs, and their carcasses washed into coastal rivers. Waste lagoons on CAFOs overflowed, sending tons of manure into the Pamlico and Core Sounds. The waste produced a dead zone in the coastal areas that caused a massive fish kill. The environmental and public health effects are still being studied today.[21]

Fifty years ago, a hurricane in the same region would not have caused the deaths of so many animals, nor would it have had the environmental impact. The solution to the "problem" of disasters and CAFOs does not involve making the rescue of farm animals a policy priority. Nor does it involve making stronger waste lagoons or creating strict building codes for CAFOs. Rather, the solution lies in changing the practices of factory farming so that animals, and the humans who share their environment, are less vulnerable.

Research Methodology

In this book, I describe recent disasters and their impact on animals, with a focus on how our understanding of those animals gives them varying moral status and thus varying vulnerability. The data come largely from interviews and published materials. I supplement these data with ethnographic data from field work conducted in the staging area for the rescue of animals from New Orleans following Hurricane Katrina, and from participant observation in disaster response volunteer training. In the Katrina research, I traveled with three staff members from the Humane Society of Boulder

Valley to assist in the sheltering operation at Lamar-Dixon Exhibition Center in Gonzales, Louisiana. The four of us had experience working in large sheltering facilities. Our role was to assist in caring for the more than two thousand dogs, one hundred cats, and numerous other animals housed at Lamar-Dixon. During September 2005, Lamar-Dixon was the largest functioning animal shelter in the United States. Over a thousand volunteers came from all over the country to staff the facility. They included animal control officers, veterinarians and veterinary technicians, shelter workers, and people who simply wanted to help. My team and I spent six days working from dawn until after dark, feeding dogs, cleaning kennels, preparing dogs for transfer out of Louisiana, and generally doing any work involved with that massive rescue effort. As I worked, I held field conversations with other volunteers, which I wrote up in extensive notes each evening.

One cannot plan disaster research in the ways other research can be planned. Moreover, disaster-related data are highly perishable. One cannot go back and study the staging area for a rescue once it is no longer operating. Consequently, some of the evidence for this book comes from interviews I have conducted with rescuers, volunteers, and other who experienced various disasters. For example, in July 2004, I had a long conversation over lunch with Sally Matluck, who had been instrumental in setting up the first MASH unit for animals following Hurricane Andrew, which struck Dade County, Florida, in 1992. About a month after that conversation, Hurricane Charley struck Charlotte County, Florida, on the southwest coast. I traveled to that area a week later and observed the devastation in Punta Gorda, Port Charlotte, and environs. I interviewed the director of Animal Control for Charlotte County and the director of the Suncoast Humane Society, which was the staging area for the response. Both were the key players in what turned out to be a highly organized and effective animal response effort. In other cases, I have relied on interviews published in print or on Web pages. I also make extensive use of reports and manuals designed for field responders, training materials, and other similar materials. In addition, I have analyzed the content of over nine hundred articles related to animals in disasters that appeared in national newspapers and were located through LexisNexis.

I use these materials to examine how disaster response decisions regarding animals are made, and by whom. I focus on how the sociozoologic scale influences how institutions consequently "think," in Mary Douglas's use of the term, about the needs of animals and about organizational roles in the disaster response.[22] I use the idea of institutional "thinking" as a metaphor for the interpretive practices that appear in discourse. Institutions "think" for those within their purview by offering models through which experience is processed. As a guiding metaphor, institutional "thinking" reveals how the discourse and activities of a group or organization produce and reproduce characteristic definitions of and solutions to the problems within their scope.[23] In the chapters that follow, I discuss how institutional thinking justified both the spending of over $80,000 per animal on rehabilitating sea otters following the *Exxon Valdez* oil spill and the bulldozing of live chickens trapped in battery cages after a tornado.

What Is a Disaster?

Thinking about disasters begins with questions about hazards. Hazards can be defined as sources of danger that may lead to emergencies or disasters. Hazards are inescapable realities of living in the physical world. They are intrinsic to the natural and built environments. Many hazards occur exclusively or most frequently in specific regions or times. Earthquakes occur along fault lines. The midwestern United States has earned the nickname "tornado alley," and the designated hurricane season runs from June through early November. Emergency management involves assessing risk, or the likelihood that a hazard will occur. When a risk is realized, the result can be an emergency, which is an unexpected incident that creates the need for an immediate response that can usually be addressed by local fire, police, animal control, or other entities. When the incident exceeds the capacity of local resources to respond, it is considered a disaster. Both kinds of events can harm lives and property and disrupt "normal" life.

When local and state agencies lack or lose the resources to respond, a governor may request that the President declare a major disaster. The request is prepared jointly by state officials and staff members from one of the ten regional offices of the Federal Emergency Management Agency (FEMA). After consideration at the regional level, the staff at FEMA's Washington, DC, headquarters reviews the request. FEMA then makes a recommendation to the President. The presidential declaration activates numerous resources through twenty-seven federal departments and agencies, which are coordinated through FEMA under the Federal Response Plan. Federal assistance is intended to supplement state and local efforts. FEMA and other federal agencies do not take control of disasters; the governor and local officials maintain oversight and control of relief efforts.

Disaster response is coordinated through the National Incident Management System (NIMS) and the National Response Plan. The NIMS orchestrates the activities of local, state, federal, and tribal governments and standardizes the practices for the response through the National Response Plan.[24] According to the Department of Homeland Security, the National Response Plan

> establishes a single, comprehensive framework for the management of domestic incidents. It provides the structure and mechanisms for the coordination of Federal support to State, local, and tribal incident managers and for exercising direct Federal authorities and responsibilities. The NRP [National Response Plan] assists in the important homeland security mission of preventing terrorist attacks within the United States; reducing the vulnerability to all natural and man-made hazards; and minimizing the damage and assisting in the recovery from any type of incident that occurs.[25]

The National Response Plan categorizes the kinds of assistance needed into emergency support functions, such as firefighting, housing, communication, and transportation, and support annexes, which provide administrative assistance. In addition, a series of incident annexes detail plans for specific events, such as biological terrorism, nuclear accident, or an oil and hazardous materials accident. For example, the Food and Agriculture Annex outlines a coordinated federal response to incidents involving food and livestock.

There are many different types of disasters, and some that uniquely affect animals. Disasters can be roughly categorized as natural or technological. Natural disasters include hurricanes, tornadoes, blizzards, extreme heat, flood, fire, and drought, as well as geological incidents, such as earthquakes, landslides, tsunamis, and volcanoes. Technological disasters include fires, nuclear accidents, and incidents involving hazardous material or biological or chemical weapons. In this category, too, are the hazards posed by terrorist attacks, bombings, power blackouts, and computer viruses. In addition, biohazards pose significant risks to animals through large-scale disease outbreaks, such as avian flu, foot-and-mouth disease (FMD), and bovine spongiform encephalopathy, or mad cow disease. Hazards often overlap in disasters; for example, an earthquake or flood may create technological risks when containers of chemicals are damaged and seep into land or water. Moreover, as this book makes clear, different species or "categories" of animals face different risks. Livestock and wildlife are at risk for biohazards, such as disease. Their status as commodities places different value on their lives. Companion animals face the risk of abandonment following flood or fire. Captive marine species rely on electricity to make their water environment habitable, and electrical power is often lost during disasters. Most of the ten thousand fish in the Aquarium of the Americas, for example, did not survive after New Orleans lost power and the aquarium's generator failed. Penguins, sea otters, and other animals were transported to other facilities. In short, how we use animals largely determines the kinds of risk they encounter.

Who Responds? What Happens to Animals during Disasters?

There is no Red Cross for animals. The U.S. Department of Agriculture, which oversees numerous issues related to animals in food production and research laboratories, has neither money nor mandate to provide for animals in disasters.[26] The United States has no comprehensive plan for zoos and marine parks (although most have individual plans). When declared national disasters involve animals, the response typically involves a patchwork of organizations and individuals, including local and state veterinarians, departments of agriculture and public health, humane societies, local emergency managers, animal control agencies, animal shelter administrators, kennel clubs, breeders, equestrian groups, concerned citizens, and others considered animal stakeholders. The incident and the type of animals involved influence who responds. Different events within the same animal population also determine who responds, and how.[27] For example, an outbreak of a disease among livestock would involve state and local veterinarians and, in some cases, the state department of agriculture.[28] It would also bring in the U.S. Department of Agriculture's Animal and Plant Health Inspection Service. The response would involve euthanasia of affected animals and "pre-emptive slaughter" of others. The disease agent would determine the appropriate measures to safely dispose of carcasses and sanitize soil. Carcass disposal can raise public health and environmental issues, including odor and pollution. Depending on the cause of the disaster, officials from the Environmental Protection Agency and the Department of Natural Resources might monitor disposal.

An occurrence of livestock disease could easily become a disaster. For example, the 2001 outbreak of FMD paralyzed Britain's agricultural infrastructure and cost the equivalent of $12 billion. The outbreak resulted in the "depopulation" of over four million cows, pigs, and sheep, the majority of whom lived in affected areas but were not infected with the disease. The economic impact included direct costs such as lost animals, carcass disposal, and response and eradication efforts. When meat processing was suspended, workers employed in slaughterhouses lost jobs. Hauling companies and rendering facilities experienced dramatic downturn. The outbreak also caused significant indirect costs to tourism and trade in Great Britain and western Europe, as well, when travel was restricted to control the spread of the disease. Many small businesses in the affected areas, such as pubs and inns, closed. The economic ripple effect is estimated at $150 million a week. In addition, the outbreak had nonmonetary consequences. Some of the animals in Great Britain were "legacy" herds, raised by particular families for generations. Depopulation on an unprecedented scale meant the loss of a way of life. As one farmer explained, "To see your life's work lying dead in your yards and fields is something no one can imagine until you see it for yourself."[29] As researchers point out, in rural communities, "sending animals for slaughter may be routine under normal circumstances, but during FMD it happened in an indiscriminate way on a massive scale. It was sometimes cruel and poorly managed and, more importantly, it happened in the back yard of the farmers and their children—in front of their very eyes." Farm families in stricken areas were ostracized, and over eighty suicides were reported among farmers and other animal stakeholders affected by the outbreak.[30]

If we consider the same herd of livestock but change the scenario to an outbreak of a zoonotic disease or one that can spread to the human population, the response would involve public health officials in addition to the agencies already mentioned.[31] Emerging zoonoses, such as the H5N1 strain of avian flu, have potentially serious impact on human health and the global economy.[32] The response would also involve euthanasia, "pre-emptive slaughter," and carcass disposal. Finally, still considering the same animals but changing the scenario to an animal disease that is foreign to the United States or to North America (known as foreign animal disease, or FAD), an outbreak would bring worldwide attention and response. FADs have significant and even devastating impact on the livestock industry. Because they can affect trade on an international level, the World Trade Organization oversees FADs through the World Organization for Animal Health. As a member of the World Trade Organization, the United States monitors FADs through the Department of Agriculture's Animal and Plant Health Inspection Services.[33]

The decision-making process and other aspects of the response vary by incident and by the type of animals affected. I begin with the most familiar: companion animals, and in the first chapter examine the response following Hurricane Katrina. Then, in the chapters that follow, I discuss situations that may be less familiar to readers. Specifically, I examine animals raised for food, marine birds and wildlife, and animals in research labs. My goal is to show that although we must incorporate animals into existing response plans, it makes better moral and economic sense to reduce animals' vulnerability in the long term.

I want to make one final point before going further. This book is not about animal rights. It is about animal *welfare*, and I want to make the distinction clear. From the perspective of rights, animals have the right not to be treated as "things," particularly as the property of others. Thus, we cannot confine them for food, entertainment, companionship, or clothing. We cannot breed them to serve as research subjects. Implementing the rights perspective would abolish many of the institutionalized uses of animals. In doing so, we would indeed eliminate many of the conflicts in disaster response, especially the one about whether to save humans or animals. As Gary Francione writes:

> If we recognize that animals have a basic right not to be treated as our resources, and we abolish those institutions of animal exploitation that assume that animals are nothing but our resources just as we abolished human slavery, we will stop producing animals for human purposes and thereby eliminate the overwhelming number of these false conflicts in which we must "balance" human and animal interests. *We will no longer drag animals into the burning house, and then ask whether we should save the human or the animal.* (Emphasis in the original.)[34]

I agree that not treating animals as our property would solve many of our existing human-animal conflicts, including many of those in disaster policy. But my aims in this book are more practical. I recognize that animals and their products play an enormous role in the economy. I understand that, at most, only about 3 percent of the U.S. population lives on a plant-based diet. I also understand that most people associate the idea of "animal rights" with the blood-tossing antics of People for the Ethical Treatment of Animals and thus see the entire movement, and the idea, as extremist. Consequently, I take a welfarist perspective that acknowledges our deeply entrenched uses of animals and attempts to see that the animals "are healthy and have what they want."[35] This is the simplest, most straightforward definition of *welfare*. I take a welfarist perspective because I recognize the conditions that exist and hope to improve the situation of animals within them. By incorporating welfare considerations into our existing uses of animals, we also reduce vulnerability—overall and during disasters. I believe we can accomplish this goal without imposing undue hardships on people. In this book, I suggest numerous ways we can do so.

We have brought billions of animals into existence to satisfy our pleasures, our needs, and our appetites. For a long time, it was impossible for us to step outside our position of dominance and ask what moral obligations we have to those animals. Recently, however, the tide has begun to turn. More people are asking whether the animals in a given situation "are healthy and have what they want." More people are recognizing that all living beings are connected, that we are all vulnerable. Thus, the time is right to begin to question and reform our uses of animals. Doing so does not mean that we will eliminate all situations in which animals need rescue, but it will eliminate the majority of such situations. I realize this will seem like a radical proposal. I hope the evidence that follows will convince you that it is also sensible.

1 / Companion Animals

> Let us not, however, flatter ourselves overmuch on
> account of our human victories over nature. For each
> such victory nature takes its revenge on us.
>
> FRIEDRICH ENGELS, *DIALECTICS OF NATURE* (1883)

As residents of New Orleans prepared for the Hurricane Gustav evacuation in August 2008, the city's Offices of Emergency Preparedness provided buses to take residents without transportation to Red Cross shelters. Additional shelters were ready to accommodate their companion animals, and trucks were on hand to transport them. Evacuees received wristbands with identification numbers that matched those on collars placed on their animals. The buses took human evacuees to a shelter in Shreveport, near the Louisiana State Fairgrounds, which was transformed into what became known as the Mega Shelter for the region's animals. The transportation and identification systems, and the shelters for people and animals in proximity, were the results of lessons learned in Hurricane Katrina. But in September, when Hurricane Ike struck Galveston Island, Texas, the situation was dramatically different. Around half of the island's residents left their animals behind when they evacuated, despite instructions to take their animals with them. The governor had made it possible for evacuees to take their animals on public transportation. Even so, rescuers found more than eight hundred abandoned animals on Galveston Island, including many tied up or left in crates.[1] The lessons learned after Hurricane Katrina, when thousands of animals were abandoned, seem to have been easily forgotten, even just a few hundred miles away.

Hurricane Katrina struck Louisiana just after six A.M. on Monday, August 29, 2005. This was the storm's second landfall. It had come ashore on the southeast coast of Florida four days earlier as a category 1 hurricane. It brought heavy rainfall and winds up to seventy miles an hour. It uprooted trees and did some structural damage. Many areas lost power. It lost some strength as it traveled across the Florida peninsula but became a category 3 hurricane over the Gulf of Mexico.[2]

On August 27, the Louisiana Society for the Prevention of Cruelty to Animals (LA/SPCA) in New Orleans evacuated its 250 adoptable animals to the Houston SPCA in climate-controlled trucks. The New Orleans facility, located on Japonica Street in the Ninth Ward, was prone to flooding, and its emergency plan called for evacuation for hurricanes of category 3 or above. Twenty-five dogs who were being held at the LA/SPCA as evidence in court cases, a common occurrence in animal sheltering, could legally not leave the state. They were evacuated to Baton Rouge. The eighty or so animals housed at the Humane Society of Louisiana, located near the Superdome, were evacuated to Tylertown, Mississippi, about two hours north of New Orleans. A few months earlier, in what would turn out to be extraordinarily good planning, the Humane Society had purchased a plot of land with a house on it to use as a "future" hurricane evacuation site. Staff christened it "Camp Katrina."

The transfer of adoptable animals to other facilities occurs regularly in animal sheltering. It is labor-intensive, involving lots of muscle, patience, and paperwork at both the departure and arrival ends. The process had worked well in other recent hurricanes. For example, before Hurricane Charley, which hit southwest Florida in August 2004, the Suncoast Humane Society in Englewood transferred its one hundred cats and fifty dogs to shelters outside the storm's predicted path, making room to accommodate animals left homeless after the storm.[3] The transfer of animals out of New Orleans was unique because of the large numbers. During the 2005 hurricane season, transfers of this size would become common-place as rescue organizations sought to find refuge for animals left homeless first by Katrina and later by Wilma and Rita.

An August 27 press release issued by the LA/SPCA informed the public that the animals would be brought back to New Orleans on Tuesday, August 30, weather permitting. The statement advised residents who planned to evacuate the city to take their companion animals with them. It gave basic recommendations, such as making certain that animals had identification. It also cautioned: "Pets cannot survive if left to fend for themselves or tied to a stationary object. Those people who choose to abandon their pets will be charged with cruelty to animals."[4] In retrospect, the presumptuous-ness of this claim seems almost laughable. Flood waters destroyed the LA/SPCA, along with twenty other animal shelters in the Gulf Coast region. The residents who abandoned their animals num-bered in the thousands. If any charges were to have been filed, it is still unclear who would stand accused.

While the LA/SPCA staff worked, the warm waters of the Gulf Stream's Loop Current intensified the storm. Through a normally occurring phenomenon known as the "eyewall replacement cycle," it doubled in size. By August 28, it had escalated to a category 5.[5] Before its landfall in Buras-Triumph, Louisiana, in Plaquemines Parish, storm surges had already battered the area with twelve- to fourteen-foot tides and over ten inches of rain. Katrina struck as a category 3 storm. It then traveled over southeastern Louisiana and into the Breton Sound, making a third and final landfall near the border of Louisiana and Mississippi. It maintained hurricane strength well into Mississippi before dissipating while on its path toward the Great Lakes.

On Sunday, August 28, when Katrina reached category 5 sta-tus, Mayor C. Ray Nagin ordered the evacuation of New Orleans. Mandatory or voluntary evacuation orders had already been issued for much of coastal Louisiana and Mississippi. Nagin told New Orleaneans that they were "facing a storm that most of us have long feared."[6] Storm surges predicted at twenty-eight feet or more would overflow the city's levees, causing major flooding and many fatalities.[7] By Monday, August 29, several levees had been breached and the city was experiencing widespread flooding, especially in the areas to the south of Lake Pontchartrain. Residents had no power, telephone, or drinking water. Most of the city's 485,000 residents left before the airport closed and water engulfed major routes out of the region. An estimated 50,000 stayed behind, however, for numerous reasons. Many simply had no transportation.[8] Some believed their homes would adequately protect them; others did not think the aftermath would bring such destruction. Many who remained were eventually rescued from rooftops. Tragically, some died in their attics.

There are no precise figures on how many stayed behind because they would not leave their animals. In a survey of 680 Katrina evacuees staying in Houston shelters, only 9 percent cited not wanting to leave pets as the reason they did not evacuate before the hurricane.[9] The tremendous number of stray and abandoned animals reveals, however, that many of the residents who evacuated New Orleans did leave their companion animals behind, despite print and televised instructions not to do so. Media accounts made it clear that some residents were forced, under threat of arrest, to leave without their dogs and cats. Residents rescued in boats, helicopters, and emergency vehicles report that responders insisted that they would take only people, not animals.

Approximately twenty-five thousand residents who could not leave New Orleans planned to weather the storm in the Superdome, which had been designated a "shelter of last resort." The Superdome had served the same function during two previous hurricanes. Many people expected to be there for a day or two.[10] As more people converged on the facility, which had no power or water, conditions became unbearable and even dangerous. On the morning of August 29, the roof began to peel off and rain poured in. On August 30, Kathleen Blanco, the governor of Louisiana, ordered a complete evacuation of New Orleans. Those at the Superdome were to be taken to the Reliant Astrodome in Houston. Residents who brought their dogs and cats to the Superdome were forced to leave them behind when they evacuated the facility because animals are not permitted on public transportation. Numerous media accounts brought the animals' plight to public attention by describing National Guardsmen letting dogs and cats run free as their guardians watched helplessly. One of the most famous—and heart-breaking—accounts involves a little white dog named Snowball being torn from a boy's arms. As Mary Foster, of the Associated Press, reported:

> At the front of the line, the weary refugees waded through ankle-deep water, grabbed a bottle of water from state troopers and happily hopped on buses that would deliver them from the horrendous conditions of the Superdome. At the back end of the line, people jammed against police barricades in the rain. Refugees passed out and had to be lifted hand-over-hand overhead to medics. Pets were not allowed on the bus, and when a police officer confiscated a little boy's dog, the child cried until he vomited. "Snowball, Snowball," he cried.[11]

The account of Snowball brought public attention to the animals' situation, transforming what might have been merely an incident into a story. In sociological terms, Foster's piece was a critical element in the rhetorical process that turned a situation into a social problem. If dogs are simply not allowed on buses, the situation gets little coverage. But if police officers are snatching dogs from the arms of crying little boys, then it becomes a media event. Portrayed in this way, Foster's story yielded a negative image of law enforcement and, intentionally or otherwise, aroused public sympathy for the animals. From then on, the media had a critical role in raising public awareness about their situation in Katrina's aftermath. There would be no shortage of material for stories.

The Ernst N. Morial Convention Center was supposed to be a dropping-off place where residents could await transportation out of the city. However, as New Orleans police captain M. A. Pfeiffer told reporters, "The problem was, the transportation never came."[12] Tired of waiting, evacuees broke into the Convention Center and, by September 3, about twenty thousand people had sought shelter there, amid violence and unsanitary conditions. Carlos and Dale Menendez were among them. The two had stayed in their home with their white German shepherd, Lily. They were initially relieved that the city had been spared a direct hit by the hurricane. When their home flooded, they held out for three days before being rescued in a boat. Along with Lily, they were taken to a holding area where they waited for a bus that would take them to a location that, although unclear, mattered little at the time. After seven hours, the bus arrived. They begged the driver to allow Lily on board, and her sweet disposition helped persuade him. They ended up at the Convention Center, where they would spend the next five days without food or water. When the National Guard helicopters finally arrived, Dale was so weak they placed her on a stretcher for transportation. As the couple was preparing for evacuation, the National Guardsmen refused to take Lily. As the LA/SPCA recorded the story:

> The National Guard tells the family that they can't take Lily. If you keep Lily you can't be rescued. Either she stays or you don't go. They plead with the guardsmen to take Lily. They can't imagine leaving her behind. But of course their pleas go unanswered. Relaying their experience even now, Dale can hardly bear to recount it. Everyday she's haunted with the recurring image of hearing her own cries and screams as she lay on a stretcher, seeing Lily released by the guardsmen and running away from the Convention Center, alone and confused. "Oh my God, I just about lost it," Dale recalls.[13]

A far more shocking story comes from St. Bernard Parish. Several residents evacuated or were rescued from their homes and took refuge in three local schools. Many had done as instructed by taking their companion animals with them. Jodi Jones, a resident of St. Bernard Parish, later explained, "We thought we were doing a good thing by taking our animals to the school." However, when residents were evacuated from the schools in early September, "the rules changed," as CNN's Anderson Cooper put it. Jones recalled: "The deputies told us, 'If you want to get out alive, you have to go now. We're saving people, not animals.'" One evacuee, Carol Hamm, said: "People were there with dogs, cats and birds, too. You name it, people brought them. There was an old woman who wanted to take her Yorkie [Yorkshire terrier]. The dog was so tiny she could fit it in her purse. They made her leave it."[14] Rather than transporting the animals to safety, Parish deputies shot and killed the dogs and cats left in their care. The reported numbers vary between thirty-five and forty. Once the deputies had killed the animals at the schools, they went into the street to kill strays.

David Leeson Jr., a photographer for the *Dallas Morning News*, was on assignment in St. Bernard Parish. He and the reporter accompanying him were searching for a dog who was the subject of a photo Leeson had taken that conveyed the plight of the region's animals. Known only as "Oily Dog," the small dog, perhaps a Lhasa apso, sits alone, coated with oil from a St. Bernard Parish refinery. Leeson had returned to St. Bernard's to find "Oily Dog." As he stopped to help another dog wandering the streets, police officers drove up in two vehicles and shot the dog. Leeson recorded the incident on videotape and then began to interview Deputy Mike Minton, then of the St. Bernard Parish sheriff's office, about what he was doing. Leeson asked Minton how many dogs he had killed. Minton replied, "Enough." In late September and early October, Anderson Cooper gave the incident wide exposure on CNN.[15] David Leeson's videotape became evidence in an investigation by the Louisiana attorney general. The case eventually went to court, and the new attorney general, Buddy Caldwell, dismissed all charges of animal cruelty against Minton and Sergeant Chip Englande.

In addition to the shootings on the street, as many as thirty-three dogs and cats were shot execution style at P.G.T. Beauregard Middle School. Carol Hamm had evacuated to the high school while her husband and son took their four dogs to Beauregard Middle School by boat. Sheriff's deputies assured them they would take the dogs to an animal shelter. The two then paddled to the high school and were evacuated with Hamm the following day. When Hamm later returned to search for the dogs, she found evidence of a massacre at the school. "It's the worst memory I'll ever have," she said. "The bodies were being removed. It was horrible. I was crying over strangers' dogs. Only three of our dogs were in the room. We saw a golden retriever, two Yorkshire terriers, all breeds, and a lot of pits and rotties [pit bull terriers and Rottweilers]. Some were shot running, one up the stairs. Bullet, our husky mix, was shot in the head."[16] Physical and forensic evidence reveals that the animals were not killed humanely, with a shot to the head, but were shot in body cavities and left to bleed to death. The case remains unprosecuted.

Evacuees all over the city report being told that their animals would be rescued later. Some thought they could soon return for their animals themselves. Many residents have never returned. Not all the stories, however, are grim. On Wednesday, August 30, rescuers began evacuating patients and staff stranded in New Orleans hospitals. Several staff members at the Lindy Boggs Medical Center went to the facility to ride out the storm. They had been given permission to bring their companion animals with them. When the center flooded on September 2, the staff was evacuated, leaving the animals behind. Media accounts are unclear about the source of the orders to leave the animals but they agree that James Riopelle, an anesthesiologist, remained at the hospital with nearly seventy animals under orders to euthanize them. Ignoring the orders, he remained without power or water, amid the stench of waste and decomposing human bodies, to care for the animals until rescuers arrived five days later.[17]

The Rescue Operation

As Katrina approached the Gulf Coast, animal response teams from all over the country were staging near Baton Rouge and Jackson, Mississippi. But in the wake of violence, federal and state authorities prohibited rescuers from entering New Orleans. Finally, on September 4, the first teams were allowed into the city. Rescuers caught stray animals and broke into homes to capture others. They established feeding stations for the dogs and cats roaming the streets. In the days following the evacuation, hundreds of evacuees had called hotlines at animal welfare organizations to arrange for the rescue of animals they had left behind. The staff at Petfinder.com, the adoption database, created the Animal Response Emergency Network to accept requests for rescue and lost-and-found reports. Dozens, if not hundreds, of Web sites and blogs overflowed with pleas to rescue beloved dogs, cats, birds, and other animals.

With the New Orleans area animal shelters destroyed, there was nowhere to house the animals. With the help of the Humane Society of the United States, the LA/SPCA established a staging area for the animal rescue at the Lamar-Dixon Exposition Center in Gonzales, about forty miles away.[18] On arrival, animals received veterinary examinations and treatment, decontamination baths, if necessary, and much-needed food and water. Under normal circumstances, Lamar-Dixon hosts equestrian and livestock events. Its barns with running water and power made it an ideal site for the animal response. In addition, its three-hundred-space RV park and restrooms could accommodate the thousands of responders who would converge on the site during September and October. According to the Humane Society, 6,036 animals, mostly dogs, were rescued and cared for at Lamar-Dixon, making it the nation's largest functioning animal shelter. Volunteers came from all over the country. They included animal control officers, veterinarians and veterinary technicians, shelter workers, and "ordinary" people like me.

Because of my experience in animal handling gained through my work at the Humane Society of Boulder Valley, combined with my professional interests in the effects of disasters on animals, I had told the director of the Humane Society that I wanted to help if the facility got involved in the response. She understood that my efforts would inform a research project. I anticipated helping take in transferred animals or doing a related low-key task. I arrived at the Humane Society for my usual volunteer shift on Monday, September 12. Around 10 A.M., the volunteer coordinator rushed me to the director's office. I learned that a small group of staff members was leaving that afternoon to assist with the sheltering operation in Louisiana. The manager of a shelter in Denver had been sent there and needed help with the challenge of housing the overwhelming number of animals. The group would fly to Jackson, Mississippi, where they would meet an animal control officer driving an RV down from Cincinnati. Could I be ready to join them in two hours?

My first telephone call was to my husband, for whom this trip meant caring for our own house full of animals. Always supportive, he sent me on my way not knowing how or when I would be in contact. Thanks to two graduate students, I managed to get my classes covered. To say that I packed in a hurry is an understatement. I concentrated on the essentials and left the rest behind. Clearly, the others had done the same, because our group of four left on time. We met our new friend in Jackson and drove to Gonzales. Our role was to help care for the animals housed there.[19]

Lamar-Dixon is much like a small town. We entered through gates monitored by the National Guard. At the mention of the word *animals*, the guardsmen pointed us in a direction and, as we drove, we began to see the large rescue vehicles from the Humane Society of the United States, the American Humane Association, and other animal welfare organizations. As we approached, the noise told us we knew we were in the right place. None of us had ever heard so many dogs barking. I will never forget the noise. That night, I wrote this in my field notes:

> Who can imagine the sound of a thousand dogs barking? Until today, the question would have seemed like a perverse koan. But now that I know what a thousand dogs sound like, I wish everyone could hear. It sounds like futility, helplessness, and the desperation of this undertaking. The sound is how we knew we were near Lamar-Dixon. The grounds are vast. There are many buildings, and the military helicopters regularly drown out all else, but we eventually found the dogs by listening. The sound is simultaneously noise and music. I am sure that it will haunt me for a very long time. (9/13/05)

The Humane Society of the United States had leased five large barns for sheltering rescued animals. The barns had roofs but open sides, with five aisles of twenty stalls each. The ten-foot-by-ten-foot stalls had three walls and floors covered with wood shavings. When my team arrived on September 13, three of the five barns were full of dogs. They were all in crates, mostly of the plastic airline-type. The fourth barn housed horses, cared for by students and faculty from the Louisiana State University School of Veterinary Medicine's large animal program. The fifth barn served as the cat shelter and the veterinary hospital, staffed by the Veterinary Medical Assistance Teams. In addition, one of the three dog barns had an entire aisle of aggressive dogs; many had obviously been used for fighting. These dogs could not be kenneled with the general population and required skilled handlers.

The tremendous number of dogs led many volunteers, myself included, to wonder why there were so few cats. During the time we spent at Lamar-Dixon, there were only about fifty cats there. We hoped that because cats are more portable than most dogs, more guardians had taken their cats with them. But, we also knew that the free-roaming cats had no guardians to claim them and that many traumatized cats were simply hiding and avoiding rescuers.

When we arrived, the number of dogs at the facility was at its peak. Before September 12, state authorities would not allow animals rescued from New Orleans to be transferred out of the region. Rescue teams had been working in the city for a week, steadily bringing animals to Lamar-Dixon. The number of dogs, in particular, was staggering. After September 12, dogs who had been unclaimed since the flood could be transferred to shelters out of state, while others had to remain within Louisiana. My team and I worked in the dog shelter area from sunrise until nearly sunset. En route to Louisiana, we developed a plan whereby the three staff members would take charge of one barn each with me assisting where needed. We naively imagined implementing a system and organizing the entire operation. That first morning was a reality check. Merely cleaning the kennels in one aisle of a barn took until noon. By the time I reached halfway down the line of the 120 dogs directly in my care, more dogs had arrived. I had between three and six volunteers working with me to get them fed and watered. Meanwhile, other volunteers stationed at areas intended for bathing horses washed an endless stream of bowls. Outside, a spider web of hoses led to an area devoted to washing crates. The oppressive heat and humidity was relentless. Large fans positioned in the stalls moved some air around but also raised the noise level and filled the air with dust.

All the dogs received food and water every day, but walks were a luxury available only if we had additional volunteers. Never have I have seen dogs look so tired and stressed. The minimal paperwork taped to the kennels told the location of rescue. The record of one especially sad dog described her rescue from a house where the other two dogs were found dead, most likely of heat, thirst, and starvation. There were numerous pit bulls, but most of the dogs were mixed breeds, and most had nice dispositions, especially considering what they had endured. All were thin. Many were sick. Many had mange and diarrhea. Few of the male dogs were neutered, and numerous females were in heat. For security reasons, the Lamar-Dixon management insisted that the lights remain on in the barns overnight. Consequently, the animals had no natural day and night. The heat and humidity took a toll on the dogs, too.

Volunteers worked through the night, as vehicles arrived with rescued animals around the clock. The greatest number of animals arrived after dark, once the curfew in New Orleans forced rescue teams to leave the city. Consequently, the entire effort involved hundreds of volunteers. After September 12, when the state veterinarian allowed dogs to be transferred to shelters out of state, the transfer process added another level of work, because each dog had to receive various vaccinations to comply with health regulations. We would lead the dogs through an assembly line, holding the semblance of paperwork we had found on their kennels. At the end of the process, they were loaded into climate-controlled trucks to go to Houston, Atlanta, or other destinations. The empty kennels after the transfers gave volunteers false hope. Moments after one truckload of dogs departed for other shelters, new ones would arrive by the dozens from the streets of New Orleans.

At the entrance to the kennel area, pet owners could file reports of lost animals. Those who had made certain their animals were wearing collars and tags or microchips learned that these measures were mostly futile because the destruction of the telephone infrastructure made contacting guardians impossible. Those who came to Lamar-Dixon searching for their animals received nametags listing their first names and the types of animals they were looking for, which gave them permission to enter the barns. Looking for a lost dog could take hours, and the owners wandered up and down the aisles searching the kennels. The process was heartbreaking for everyone. As one volunteer explains:

> Something new for me today. They are letting owners of lost dogs back in to look for their dogs. They are all coming through with special nametags looking. They all look so sad and frustrated. I try to talk to some of them. "What kind of dog are you looking for," I ask. They vary in their responses. Two just start crying when I ask. I feel horrible for these people. One woman is looking for a Dachsund [sic]. I shake my head. I haven't seen one. They're not exactly the best swimmers. She starts to cry. She's the last person I ask.[20]

During my time there, I witnessed only three reunions. Each time, there was no question about how to verify the identity of the owners. In one case, while I was standing at the end of the aisle unloading dirty bowls, a dog nearby, a Border collie mix, begin to thrash and spin in his wire kennel. He yipped and squirmed, and as I went to check on him, I saw a man approaching, wearing an ear-to-ear grin. One look at him, and I knew. I opened the dog's kennel and he exploded out of it, running full-tilt toward the man. They had been separated for over two weeks. Unfortunately, the man did not find his second dog that day.

"The Magnitude and Complexity"

The LA/SPCA estimates that about twenty-three hundred of the fifteen thousand lost animals were reunited with their guardians. These numbers suggest the challenge guardians faced in trying to locate missing animals. Many of those I spoke with as they searched the aisles of Lamar-Dixon said they did not know whether their animals had been rescued or where they had been taken. Some learned about the facility only by accident.

The out-of-region and out-of-state shelters to which animals were transferred after September 13 were instructed initially to hold the animals until October 15, at which time the animals could become available for adoption to new homes. However, the major animal welfare organizations requested that the date be extended until December 15. An October 12 press release points out that the earlier date had been established "before there was a clear understanding of the magnitude and complexity of the rescue, relief and reunion operation."[21] The later deadline would give guardians more time to locate their lost animals. In the best cases, records about where an animal had been rescued traveled with the animal. But often this information was sketchy and sometimes inaccurate. A dog described as a black Lab mix who had been rescued at the intersection of two streets may have simply wandered there and not lived in the immediate vicinity at all.

Immediately after Hurricane Katrina, the online service known as Petfinder became a resource for guardians and organizations providing foster care. Petfinder provides a searchable database of adoptable animals at participating shelters. When interested adopters locate a suitable canine or feline companion online, they can access that local shelter's Web site for details about adoptions and then follow through with a visit. When Katrina struck, Petfinder's database became the platform for the Animal Emergency Response Network. With support from Maddie's Fund, a foundation dedicated to helping abandoned animals, Petfinder collaborated with animal welfare organizations involved in the rescue to post data on nearly twenty-three thousand animals from the disaster areas.[22]

The database also included nearly twenty-six thousand requests for rescue from people who left animals behind and another eight thousand lost notices. The Animal Emergency Response Network reunited thirty-two hundred animals with their human companions. The network remains in place as a public service funded by the nonprofit Petfinder to assist in future disasters.

In October 2005, the LA/SPCA leased a warehouse in the Algiers neighborhood of New Orleans to resume its operations. Because of disease control, sanitation, and safety issues, among others, establishing an animal shelter is a complicated process. With assistance from the Humane Society of the United States, the American SPCA, and regional organizations, the staff took in homeless animals while fielding telephone calls from the public and the media. In November, the LA/SPCA convened a multi-agency team to assess the state of the animals in New Orleans, particularly in the hardest hit "hot spots," including the lower Ninth Ward and St. Bernard Parish. The purpose was to estimate the number of animals at large in the city and to assess their condition. The goal was to tailor subsequent response efforts to the needs as observed. Following the assessment, national and local welfare groups sponsored a humane-trapping effort, which greatly reduced the number of strays. The number of feeding stations was reduced because of problems with rats, already rampant in the storm's aftermath.

On October 6, 2006, President George W. Bush signed the Pets Evacuation and Transportation Standards (PETS) Act into law.[23] In response to the impact of Hurricane Katrina, the PETS Act amended several sections of the Stafford Act to require state and local emergency management agencies to include companion and service animals in their disaster response plans. Funding from the Federal Emergency Management Agency (FEMA) is contingent on compliance with the PETS Act. The act had been introduced in the House of Representatives by Christopher Shays (R-CT) and the late Tom Lantos (D-CA), and in the Senate by Ted Stevens (R-AK) and Frank Lautenberg (D-NJ). The House passed its version of the act (HR 3858) in May 2006 by a vote of 349 to 24. In August, the Senate passed its version (S 2548) unanimously. The Senate amended the act in several ways. It grants FEMA the authority to assist in the creation of disaster plans for animals. It authorizes federal funds to establish pet-friendly emergency shelters. It also allows FEMA to provide aid to individuals with companion or service animals, as well as to the animals themselves. The House approved the Senate version in September. The legislation promised to enable more people to take their animals with them when forced to evacuate after a disaster. Hurricane Ike showed, however, that legislation alone does not reduce animals' vulnerability.

In December, the LA/SPCA resumed its off-site adoption program. The facility itself opened to the public in February 2006. Every few weeks it moved a new step ahead. On August 8, 2006, the LA/SPCA held a tribute to the "animals whose lives were lost or dramatically altered during Hurricane Katrina and its aftermath."[24]

What We Thought We Knew

Hurricane Katrina challenged much of the existing research on animals in disasters. What we did know ahead of time was that large numbers of animals would be affected. Surveys by the American Veterinary Medical Association indicate that 70 percent of U.S. households include dogs and cats. Add in birds and horses, and the figure surpasses 75 percent.[25] This percentage exceeds that of households that include children. Moreover, 60 percent of households with companion animals include multiple animals. Thus, for every 1,000 households affected by a disaster, approximately 1,500 animals will also be involved. Conservative calculations indicate that 281,300 of the 485,000 households in New Orleans included animals. Any incident that affects large numbers of people will affect animals, as well. An estimated 727,500 animals were affected by Katrina in the city alone. Best estimates by the LA/SPCA suggest that over 15,000 abandoned animals were rescued from the homes and streets of New Orleans. Although the number of animals who died is not known, reliable estimates place it in the thousands.

The animal tragedy after Hurricane Katrina reveals shifting constructions of victims and villains. The victims suffer harm through no fault of their own, while the villains are responsible for the harm. As scholars who study the construction of social problems point out, these categories are the product of rhetorical work.[26] Before the storm, when residents were instructed to take their animals with them, those who would leave animals behind were cast as potential villains. The possibility of their facing charges of animal cruelty simultaneously cast the animals as potential victims. Until Katrina, the literature on animals in disasters supported this rhetoric. Research associated the failure to evacuate animals with a weak human-animal bond.[27] Studies measured attachment and commitment to animals by indicators of care, such as visits to veterinarians and possession of leashes or carriers. A weaker standard of care indicated a weaker bond with an animal. People who left their animals behind were those who kept their dogs primarily outdoors or who had no carriers available to transport their cats. In sum, the literature supported the idea that those who really cared for their animals would evacuate them. During Katrina's aftermath, the victim/villain distinction became less clear. Numerous media accounts began to establish that many "villains" who abandoned their animals were actually forced to do so and thus became the "victims" of the structure of the response. For example, even those who did evacuate their animals, such as Carlos and Dale Menendez or the residents of St. Bernard Parish who took shelter in local schools, would face circumstances that made their care for their animals irrelevant. According to a Gallup Poll of adult Katrina survivors, 20 percent had to leave companion animals behind. However, because the questions did not clarify the circumstances under which they had to do so, it is unwise to attribute the evacuees' actions to the weakness of the bond they shared with their animals.

The tragic instances in which people left their animals behind occurred with alarming frequency. Nevertheless, these account for only a fraction of the animals abandoned in New Orleans. Why didn't more people take their companion animals with them? The question is not as simple as it seems. Before Katrina, research had established the refusal to leave animals as the most significant reason for failure to evacuate following a disaster, especially among households without children. Several factors make guardians of animals less likely to evacuate. First, the task of finding accommodations can be daunting. In most disasters, 60 to 80 percent of evacuees stay with friends or family.[28] For many reasons, friends and family will not or cannot accommodate companion animals. Evacuees who cannot stay with friends or family must be extremely resourceful. For health and safety reasons, companion animals (except service animals) are not allowed in Red Cross shelters. In some situations, responders establish "pet-friendly" shelters, in which accommodations for people and animals are in close proximity. A fairgrounds might house people in exhibition buildings, for example, while the barns are turned into shelters for companion animals (or livestock). In pet-friendly shelters, responders and volunteers provide primary care for the animals, but guardians can visit. After Katrina, for example, the John M. Parker Coliseum at Louisiana State University became a shelter for the animals of residents who evacuated to Baton Rouge.[29] There is no evidence, however, that the availability of pet-friendly shelters improves evacuation rates. In addition, some have argued that the arrangement may also make guardians dependent on others for the care of their animals.[30]

Researchers have found that households with animals have significantly greater difficulty finding accommodations than do those without animals. In some disasters, evacuees have stayed in their cars or at campgrounds with their animals. Previous research suggests that, in prolonged evacuations, the lack of pet-friendly accommodations "forces a significant lifestyle change on some households and could in some cases even lead to temporary homelessness."[31] Many guardians have no choice but to surrender their animals to shelters. During the year following Katrina, the Humane Society of Louisiana noted a 30 to 50 percent increase in intakes.[32] People who could not find pet friendly housing found themselves unable to provide suitable homes for their dogs and cats. In short, the issue of accommodations complicates the constructions of villain and victim. The guardian who does the right thing by evacuating with his or her animals avoids being a villain in one construction but becomes a villain later, in having to surrender the animals to a shelter.

Another factor that has been associated with evacuation failure is the lack of transportation. One researcher points out that "the major obstacles to evacuating pets appear to be logistic, resulting from an inability to transport pets."[33] After Katrina, people who owned vehicles found their cars and trucks useless when flood waters rose too high. The evacuation of New Orleans also highlighted the difficulties faced by people who rely on public transportation. At the time, animals were not allowed on buses or other public vehicles. New Orleans has since modified disaster plans to allow animals in carriers.

Guardians such as Jodi Jones and Carlos and Dale Menendez, who did the right thing and evacuated with their dogs, learned that the villains were the National Guard and local law enforcement. Acting on ill-advised policy to "save people, not animals," the military and other rescuers became the villains and then complicated the ensuing response by letting animals run free, as the National Guard had done with the Menendezes' dog, Lily. These responders made evacuees' lives more stressful and also ensured the need for a subsequent animal rescue operation of unprecedented size and complexity.

Research has already documented that leaving a companion animal behind in a disaster can pose additional health risks to evacuees already under serious strain. For example, following a tornado that struck West Lafayette, Indiana, in 1994, evacuees exhibited signs of psychological distress and medically unexplained physical symptoms from uncertainty over the safety and whereabouts of their companion animals.[34] Until Katrina, we knew nothing about the emotional and psychological consequences of being physically forced to leave an animal behind. In my work at the shelter facility for animals rescued out of New Orleans, I saw distraught guardians spending entire days searching the rows of kennels for their dogs. The few reunions I witnessed were beyond joyful on the parts of the people and the animals. Because companion animals and humans depend on each other, evacuating animals is part of caring for the needs of people.

In addition, there are public safety reasons why animals must be evacuated. Research has long documented that leaving animals behind creates additional safety risks. Residents will often put themselves at risk by re-entering evacuated areas to rescue their animals. Following a spill of phosphorus and liquid sulfur in Dayton, Ohio, in 1984, for example, residents attempting to retrieve animals created traffic jams that blocked evacuation. Risks of a more serious nature were involved following an incident in Weyauwega, Wisconsin, in 1996.[35] At 5:30 A.M. on March 4, 1996, a train derailed while passing through Weyauwega. Fifteen of the train's cars carried propane, and five of these caught fire. At 7:30, concerns about potential explosion prompted emergency responders to order the residents of Weyauwega's 1,022 households to evacuate. Emergency personnel anticipated that the response would take several hours. Fifty percent of the 241 households that included animals left them behind, believing they would not be gone for long. But because of the unpredictability of disaster response, the response took much longer. Shortly after the evacuation, 40 percent of pet owners reentered the evacuation zone illegally to rescue their pets. Following protocol, emergency managers prevented residents from attempting to enter their own homes. A group of citizens made a bomb threat "on behalf" of the animals, which directed considerable negative media attention at the response. Four days after the evacuation, the Emergency Operations Center organized an official pet rescue, supervised by the National Guard and using the guard's armored vehicles.

Following Katrina, state and federal authorities prohibited teams of professional rescuers from entering the city in a timely fashion. Using paternalistic rhetoric of protecting rescuers from violence, authorities delayed the rescue of animals and contributed to the deaths of untold numbers of dogs and cats. Animal rescue teams undergo thorough training, and all professionals and many volunteers have FEMA credentials. They understand that they are not to place themselves at unnecessary risk. Yet, the blockade of the city prevented animal response teams from doing what they had agreed to do. Government policy became the villain.

The PETS Act represents a sincere effort to change that image and to ensure that the chaos and tragedy of Katrina does not occur again. The act was championed by nearly every animal welfare and rights group in the country. By requiring states to include companion and assistance animals in their emergency plans, the act publicly recognizes the importance of the human-animal bond. It is an important part of the solution, but Ike showed that it does not eliminate the need for people to create their own disaster plans and include their animals in them. State animal response teams across the country emphasize the need for local plans, as does FEMA, the Humane Society of the United States, the American Humane Association, and every emergency response agency. The information is available to people online and in print form. The question of how to get people to act on it is complex. It is difficult enough to plan for what we know will happen tomorrow or next week. It is much more difficult to plan for something unknown, such as a disaster, which might not happen at all. In the Conclusion, I offer some ideas for how to encourage people to prepare. Legislation such as the PETS Act gives us hope but should not lull us into thinking that all is well. When we took animals into our homes, we made a contractual agreement to provide for their care. Our obligations to those who depend so completely on us do not end with a piece of legislation.

2 / Animals on Factory Farms

> The worst sin toward our fellow creatures is not to hate
> them, but to be indifferent to them: that's the essence of
> inhumanity.
>
> GEORGE BERNARD SHAW, *THE DEVIL'S DISCIPLE* (1906)

Although we have the closest bonds with companion animals, they constitute only about 2 percent of the animals living in the United States. The other 98 percent are the cattle, sheep, hogs, and poultry raised for food. According to the U.S. Department of Agriculture (USDA), ten billion such animals are raised—and killed—for food every year.[1] The conditions under which most of these animals live make them extremely vulnerable in disasters, and they pose serious environmental and public health risks under normal circumstances. Disasters highlight the conflict between consumer welfare and animal welfare. In this chapter, I suggest a way to reconcile the two sides.

While companion animals live on the borderland of the human-animal boundary, assuming a nearly human status as family members, farmed animals occupy the "animal" side, and have done so for centuries. Anthropologists point to the domestication of animals for food as a turning point in human-animal relations. As Elizabeth Lawrence puts it, "It is impossible to overestimate the importance of mankind's change from hunter-gatherer to domesticator of plants and animals."[2] The term *domestication* refers to the process by which the care, diet, and breeding of a species come under human control. Traditional hunter-gatherers considered animals their equals, and in some instances thought animals possessed religious or magical powers. That relationship changed with domestication, and, James Serpell explains, "for the majority of species involved, this loss of independence had some fairly devastating long-term consequences."[3] The changes that have occurred within livestock farming over the past fifty years have intensified those consequences.

The latter half of the twentieth century marked what scholars call the "third agricultural revolution."[4] The first revolution involved the development of seed agriculture, along with the use of the plow and draft animals, such as oxen. The second revolution brought the large-scale use of fertilizers, agrochemicals, and animal feed, purchased from suppliers off the farm. The third revolution brought industrialized agriculture, also called factory farming. Although the term *factory farming* currently has negative connotations, the agricultural industry itself introduced the term, preferring it because it implies efficient production. Factory farming involved a rapid increase of production from fewer and larger farms, as well as closer corporate involvement. For the cattle, pigs, chickens, sheep, and turkeys that we domesticated from their wild ancestors, the third revolution has meant lives deprived of the capacity to express every natural instinct. In industrialized agriculture, pigs are confined in crates that do not allow them to turn around, much less wallow in the mud or root for their food. Chickens who lay eggs do not even have the space to spread their wings. Many authors have already described the horrors of factory farming, so I will not go into detail here. However, I want to emphasize that as we humans have learned how to "grow" animals faster and more economically, we have engineered creatures useful to us only as commodities. To justify our treatment of them, we deny their cognitive and emotional capacities; more accurately, we deprive ourselves of seeing and understanding these capacities. To be sure, there are still some small farms and ranches in which farmers have frequent contact with their animals and see them as individuals.

However, in the majority of agriculture today, humans and animals have little contact. There is little "animal husbandry" involved. What contact humans and animals do have often occurs during transportation and slaughter. This state of affairs leaves little opportunity to come to understand farmed animals as sentient beings.

Farmed animals face numerous risks in disasters. Cattle and other grazing animals are affected by weather. Blizzards and floods can strand animals, making it impossible for them to get to food and water. Hypothermia poses a risk to all animals. Wind and debris in hurricanes, earthquakes, and tornadoes can cause traumatic injuries. Unusually high heat (defined as ten degrees or more Fahrenheit above the average high) can result in heat stress in cattle. They also face numerous risks from disease outbreaks, which can "depopulate" entire herds or flocks. The value of farmed animals only as commodities largely determines their treatment during disasters. There is little public outcry or support for the rescue of farmed animals after disasters. The USDA, which oversees many aspects of the animal industry, has no mandate to rescue farmed animals during disasters.[5] Farmed animals are, quite simply, not worth the trouble. When a disaster compromises the quality of the products the animals embody, consumer welfare trumps animal welfare. Thus, factory farm disasters prompt an examination of how people decide the moral worth of animals. They also encourage consideration of the way we establish and maintain the ethical boundaries that separate farmed animals from companion animals.[6] Nowhere are these issues more obvious than with chickens.

The bird we know as the chicken was domesticated from Indian and Southeast Asian red jungle fowl around 6000 BCE.[7] Flocks were first established in China, then India, Japan, and Korea. Beginning around 1200 BCE, domesticated chickens were transported through Russia to Europe and eventually to the New World. Like most other birds, chickens are highly social. They are known for the "pecking order," which refers to their complex group structure. In stark contrast to the epithet "chicken," mother hens are fiercely protective of their young and roosters are often gallant in their behavior toward hens. Chickens require and enjoy many of the same behaviors that other birds engage in, such as taking dust and sun baths. Given the opportunity, they will roost in trees, just as other birds do.

The "Old McDonald's farm" where hens, chicks, and the obligatory rooster move about in a sunny farmyard scarcely exists anymore. Farmyards such as these might provide eggs, milk, and meat for one family, but no farmer can make a living this way today. Ninety-five percent of the billions of animals annually raised for food are chickens. Most of these—an estimated nine billion—are raised for meat. The increased use of poultry in fast food and low-fat diets, combined with export demand, makes chicken the most popular meat. The production of chicken for meat has increased from just over thirty-four thousand birds in 1934 to over eight million in 2004. In 1960, the average American consumed just over nineteen pounds of chicken a year. By 2001, annual consumption had increased to over fifty-four pounds.[8]

The demand for chicken changed the way the birds are raised. Chickens were the first animals to be raised in intensive confinement. Beginning on a large scale in the 1950s, some breeds of chickens were bred exclusively for meat, rather than egg production. These breeds are known as broilers, named by the poultry industry as an end product even from birth. They spend their six-week lives in windowless sheds called grower houses. Lighting is minimized to limit aggression and reduce activity, so that all caloric intake goes to body weight rather than other energy expenditures. To be profitable, broiler operations usually house between 20,000 and 50,000 birds in a single grower house.[9] A typical operation consists of at least four such buildings. Flocks of between 150,000 to 300,000 birds are common on a single site. Even so-called free-range chicken comes from confined birds. At current consumption rates, we do not have enough land in the United States to give each bird the space required for spreading wings, much less establishing territory, nesting, dust bathing, and doing what comes naturally to chickens.

The individual farmer who raises the chickens is known as a contract grower or a producer. He or she receives chicks as young as one day old from a company that controls every aspect from breeding to "processing," or slaughter and packaging, of finished "products." Referred to as integrators, these companies are poultry complexes that orchestrate every aspect of production. The complex incorporates a feed mill, a slaughter house or processing facility, and a group of producers. The producers are responsible for "grow-out" of chicks to adult broilers ready for slaughter, which gives the birds a life-span of about forty-two days. Broiler producers raise five or six batches of chickens in a typical year.

In the United States, broiler production is concentrated among approximately forty-three integrated poultry complexes.[10] The top four firms produce more than 50 percent of the chicken raised for meat. In addition to corporate concentration, broiler chicken production is also concentrated geographically, in "a few southern states where farmers are highly dependent on contract arrangements for income and livelihood."[11] Concentrating production in warm climates eliminates the expense of heating the growing facilities.

Another three hundred million of the animals raised for food are egg-laying hens, who produce eggs for about two years, when their "spent" bodies, to use the poultry industry's term, are slaughtered for soup, school lunches, and other products containing low-quality meat.[12] All but around 5 percent of these hens spend their lives in large, windowless sheds. They live with five to eleven other hens in eighteen-inch-by-twenty-inch wire cages, known as "batteries."[13] In egg production facilities, four tiers of battery cages run the length of a warehouse. Feeding and watering is automated, and the birds are kept in darkness much of the time. The battery system significantly reduces the human labor needed to produce eggs. In the 1960s, when most flocks were still relatively small (under a thousand birds), one grower oversaw a single flock. Today, the ratio is roughly one grower for thirty thousand birds.[14] The advantages of the battery system are limited to the grower. The hens endure tremendous overcrowding, without enough room to spread a wing, much less move. Their feet are often injured by the wire mesh flooring of their cages. Their natural instinct to establish territory and a pecking order is managed by "debeaking," in which their beaks are cut off with a hot blade when the birds are just a few days old.

In both broiler and egg-laying facilities, the producers are responsible for day-to-day tasks, but the integrator owns the birds. This arrangement becomes an important factor in disaster response. Because the producers do not own the birds, they cannot legally authorize or conduct rescue operations. In addition, the huge numbers of birds and animals in a typical facility pose tremendous logistical problems with transportation and rehousing. Saving the lives of farmed animals often costs more than the monetary value of the animals' bodies. Two examples of disasters affecting chicken facilities, one for broilers and one for egg-laying hens, illustrate how the moral status of animals creates a lethal vulnerability.

"It Looked Like a Field of Cotton"

Farm Sanctuary estimates that at the time of Hurricane Katrina, 635 million farm animals were being raised in the region comprising Louisiana, Florida, Mississippi, Alabama, and Georgia. The Humane Society of the United States puts the number in the billions. The region is one of several in the country known for huge broiler production facilities. Tyson Foods produces approximately five million chickens a week just in Mississippi.[15] Sanderson Farms had 1,874 broiler houses in Mississippi at the time. The company estimates that three million broiler chickens died because of Katrina.[16]

After the storm, compared with the coverage given to companion animals, reports of farm animals injured and killed were slow to appear in the media. A tornado that struck in Katrina's wake destroyed thirty or more growing sheds in Georgia. Thousands of birds were killed, and countless other remained trapped. Wind tore the roofs from broiler facilities in Alabama and Mississippi, exposing hundreds of thousands of birds to severe weather. The storm knocked out the power in much of the region and, without electricity and locked into cages, chickens would die of starvation and thirst.

The staff of Farm Sanctuary and Animal Place, both of which rescue and shelter farmed animals, were watching reports from the region. Kate Walker, of Farm Sanctuary, and Kim Sturla, of Animal Place, went to Jackson, Mississippi, to get lists of broiler and laying facilities from the USDA and farm bureau representatives.[17] They then drove into the rural areas, often unsure where they were because any road signs or landmarks that might have guided them had been blown away. Ten days had passed, and the poultry companies were considering their broiler and layer facilities a loss. Walker and Sturla scouted the area, going from farm to farm and stopping at processing facilities, asking people where the growing houses were. Both recall that people were at first suspicious of these two women, one from New York, the other from California, who were looking for chickens. They encountered no active resistance but little cooperation, either.

As the birds died in the wrecked houses, the companies began to consider the issue one of biosecurity. The odor of manure pits mixed with that of dead and dying birds. People who lived near poultry facilities began complaining about the odor. Broiler production requires electricity for ventilation, not only because of the heat but because the concentration of birds creates an overwhelming odor of urine. Walker recalled that the odor provided a compass in a landscape where the storm had taken away the road signs. "We got to where we thought the road was," she explained, "and then we'd roll down the windows." At first, poultry companies had told farmers just to let the birds out. However, the birds ran all over neighborhoods and were hit by cars. Then, as the birds began dying of thirst, starvation, and heat, companies simply decided to bury them, even those who were still alive. Bulldozers and front-loaders arrived to level the facilities and "dispose of" the birds. By September 12, when rescue efforts on behalf of the region's dogs and cats were in full force, poultry companies had begun bulldozing chickens into mass graves. Sturla recounted the scene at the first facility she found:

> We met the farmer, and he was willing to let us take those
> that we could catch, because they were just dying out there.
> It was already, I think, ten days poststorm. [The poultry
> company] were getting their bulldozers and just bulldoz-

ing them up. They had this huge pit, which was probably twenty feet deep and then ten by ten wide and long. And they would just dispose of the bodies. And they could sometimes catch a few, but they weren't going to go out there at night. They actually did catch several thousand, but [the grower] thought that there were about five hundred remaining and it just wasn't worth it. In actuality, there were about two thousand remaining.

Soon after, Sturla's Animal Place and the Humane Society of the United States began to get calls for help from residents living near facilities where birds were decomposing. One caller reported seeing "so many dead chickens, it looked like a field of cotton." At one facility, the producer had struggled to catch and relocate fifteen thousand birds from sheds that had been, in Walker's words, "completely ripped in half," into two other sheds that were damaged but still standing. Sturla and Walker emphasized that catching birds is laborious. Because the birds are so fast, it is best done at night when the birds are somewhat calmer. The farmer understood that it was inhumane to crowd more birds into the already packed shed. He had contacted the poultry company to ask them what to do. They told him to start burying them. By this time, Walker recounted, the birds were already running "all over the place," so farm workers had to catch them individually, chasing them on all-terrain vehicles and wringing their necks. As Walker recounted:

We pulled up, and there were birds everywhere. There were thousands and thousands of birds. They were just running free. We pulled up and the farm staff was all standing there, and they kind of looked at us strangely. We explained we were from New York and California and we were there to save chickens. The farmer pulled up. We were really nervous, because we really wanted to get these birds. They were really suffering. They were tiny. Probably about two weeks old. He was glad that we were there, and said we could have all the birds we could catch.

In an exemplary illustration of the ambivalence with which we regard animals, the farmer explained that he was an "animal lover" and did not want the birds to suffer. As Walker recalls, he could not see how the birds suffered under their normal treatment as broiler hens.

In another instance, Walker describes the farm workers' efforts to spare a few birds despite burying thousands. The shells of four sheds remained standing, with carcasses everywhere. In one shed, she recalled, the floor was a foot and a half thick with carcasses. There were some live birds remaining among the dead. Walker started gathering up the injured and placing them together near water bowls that she set out, creating several islands of birds who might revive. Walker and Sturla left the facility to get supplies and planned to return at night to capture the birds. When they returned, the workers had plowed and buried the shed. However, they had taken the trouble to plow around the little islands Walker had created, sparing a few birds while burying tens of thousands of others.

With assistance from the Humane Society, Walker and Sturla rescued nearly a thousand chickens from the facility. The birds were transported to Animal Place and Farm Sanctuary, both in California, and to other sanctuaries for farmed animals. In addition, because many people are willing to adopt hens, they are easier to rescue than larger animals.

The Buckeye Farm Disaster

While companion birds such as parrots, cockatiels, and parakeets were being rescued from the homes of New Orleans, chickens were being buried alive in Mississippi. The scene repeated itself in Georgia, Alabama, Louisiana, and Florida. Hurricane Katrina, however, was only the latest example of the vulnerability posed by factory farming, particularly to chickens.

On September 20, 2000, several tornadoes destroyed twelve laying sheds at the Buckeye Egg Farm outside of Croton, Ohio.[18] At the time, the fifteen million hens held at the Buckeye facility made Ohio the largest egg-producing state in the country. Over a million birds were trapped in their mangled cages within twelve damaged sheds. The automated feed, water, and waste disposal mechanisms were destroyed. Although many birds were killed, tens of thousands of others had no chance to escape death from starvation, thirst, and exposure. The owners of the farm would not provide the funds or the labor to rescue the birds, nor would they initially allow rescuers to do so. Buckeye Egg Farms was already notorious for environmental and safety violations.[19] Allowing rescuers in would allow outsiders to see the appalling conditions in which the chickens lived.

The day after the tornado, Cayce Mell and Jason Tracy, of the OohMahNee Farm, a sanctuary in western Pennsylvania, went to Buckeye Farms to rescue the birds. OohMahNee could house several hundred chickens. However, thousands could easily be saved from the wreckage. Mell called on other animal rescue organizations. Lorri Bauston, then of Farm Sanctuary, committed to taking twelve hundred birds, bringing the numbers potentially rescued to two thousand. The Humane Society provided a grant to help defray the costs of rescue and issued a press report that brought media attention to the horrors at the Buckeye facility. Other sanctuaries and rescue groups, such as Animal Place, committed to taking birds and sent volunteers to the site. Citing "safety concerns," Buckeye's owner would not allow rescuers to take any birds, even though many birds could easily have been rescued without risk. After three days of pleading, he agreed to allow rescuers to take birds. But he would not allow them to handle the birds or touch the cages. As Lorri Bauston recalls,

> There was no serious commitment on the owner's part to get the animals out of cages. And Buckeye would not allow animal activists to do the job either. Pretty much the only thing we activists could do was to provide vehicles and transportation for rescued birds. Attempts to rescue the birds ourselves was met by stiff resistance from Buckeye. Every time we tried to grab birds from the cages, security would come after us. By the fourth day, security ringed the facility and kept all activists away.[20]

The rescuers again pleaded with Buckeye to remove the living birds to sheltered areas where they could receive food and water. Buckeye declared that only company workers were allowed to rescue birds and sent six workers to each shed. Although this action was intended as a display of concern, the reality was that each team of six employees would be tasked with the impossible job of rescuing over a hundred thousand birds. Buckeye set up one rescue area, but the majority of the birds, living and dead, were thrown into front-end loaders and packed into dumpsters. Bauston describes the scene:

> I watched what the Buckeye Egg Farm called their "rescue" operation. The "bird removal crew" consisted of six to eight workers—6 to 8 people to remove almost 100,000 birds from piles of debris and mangled cages. It was agonizingly slow . . . and cruel. The workers grabbed the birds by the legs and threw them into a tractor loading bucket. The tractor then drove to a large trailer, and dumped the live birds into it. The birds fell, flapping their wings and screaming, onto the other birds in the trailer, who lay dead, or dying. A tarp was then pulled over the trailer, and CO_2 gas was pumped into it for 5 minutes. When the tarp was pulled back, many of the birds lay gasping—until the next loader full of birds was dumped on top of them.[21]

Just as Walker had observed the workers bulldozing around a few small islands of living birds after Katrina, the workers at Buckeye displayed different attitudes toward the birds when rescuers were present. As Susie Coston of Farm Sanctuary recalls:

> We were showing [the workers] how we hold the birds. The workers tended to grab them by the legs and swing them out and hold them upside down, which is very disturbing, especially if the birds are injured. It can just cause further injury. They handle them as a product. They don't handle them as a bird. So, the people who were coming from the

animal rights groups were actually showing the workers how to carry the birds, and they were doing it. So it's not like they were all these evil people. I mean it was horrible, the work they did there. But at the same time, with us there, they did it differently.[22]

By September 28, rescuers had persuaded camera crews from ABC and Associated Press to cover the story. Buckeye officials agreed to allow filming on the premises. In a public relations display, William Glass, the chief operating officer of Buckeye, told an Associated Press reporter, "Our biggest situation is to reach these chickens and end their pain and suffering."[23] On September 29, Buckeye issued a press release announcing that because of "worker safety" concerns, it would no longer remove hens from cages. This turned out to be a cover story, as Farm Sanctuary and other groups learned that OSHA did not share these concerns. Photos and films taken by rescuers and members of the public began circulating and, two days later, Buckeye decided to allow the rescue to continue. By this time, the hens had been trapped for eleven days. Surprisingly, many were still alive and alert. Bauston recalls: "On my last trip to the Buckeye Egg Farm, the birds had been in the cages without food or water for twelve days. I expected to see birds weak and near death—what I saw instead were birds very much alive and moving frantically in their cages whenever I approached them." Buckeye was allowing rescuers to take only robust hens. They would not allow hens considered spent to leave the property, perhaps because it would further expose the horrific state of the birds. By October 1, the rescue effort had become economically impractical for Buckeye. The company ended the rescue and brought in demolition equipment to clear out the wreckage. Over half a million hens, still trapped alive in their cages, were crushed to death or buried alive.

Despite resistance, rescuers saved about five thousand birds during their week-long effort. Approximately six hundred went to live at Farm Sanctuary's New York shelter, while the rest went to other sanctuaries and adoptive homes. Walker reported that although the majority of the birds had succumbed to health problems since their rescue, many were still doing well when I spoke with her in February 2007.

Reducing Vulnerability through Sustainability

A LexisNexis search of national newspapers for articles on farm animals and disasters that I undertook during my research for this chapter illustrated the relative worth of different species. When I searched using "pets," "dogs," "cats," and "Katrina," I found over five hundred articles, but when I used "chickens" and related terms, the search produced only two articles. More than thirty years ago, Peter Singer noted that farm animals receive less media attention than other type of animal. The same is true today.[24] Farm animals are what Carol Adams calls "absent referents."[25] Unlike the abandoned dogs and cats who were portrayed as unique individuals, farm animals seldom have stories. They are simply "meat" when alive, and "units" or "losses" when they die in any way other than in the slaughterhouse. Because in neither instance are these animals that are raised for food considered living beings, we can dissociate ourselves from the suffering entailed by their treatment.

The positions of the rescuers, the poultry companies, and the farmers and workers who handled the birds also point to how the claims made about the status of farmed animals vary. Sturla emphasized the similarity between chickens and other animals, expressing frustration with the efforts exerted on behalf of companion animals. "There is sympathy for saving dogs and cats and other mammals," she explained, "but when it comes to birds, particularly chickens, that is often scoffed at and mocked." I asked her how she responds to questions about why anyone should "bother" rescuing chickens. She explained that she considered the value of life, regardless of species. As she told the *San Francisco Chronicle*, "I'm looking at it from the perspective of their lives. . . . The life of the chicken is as important to him as the life of the dog or cat is to them."[26]

Rescuers see chickens as having inherently valuable lives. They argue that the same effort should be exerted to rescue chickens as dogs or cats. They point out how even birds who have never seen the light of day will display natural behaviors soon after rescue. They will stretch their wings, take dust baths, and walk for the very first time. Despite their enjoying these simple pleasures, the reality is that chickens bred for eggs or meat will suffer health problems. For example, rescuing a "broiler chicken" to live out a "normal" life raises the question about what, because of the bird's genetically altered body, a "normal" life would be. "Broilers" are bred to reach slaughter weight at six or seven weeks of age, although they often live five or six years after rescue. Those who go into sanctuary typically have health problems related to selective breeding for unnaturally fast growth. The birds often suffer foot and leg deformities and joint problems because their bones cannot support the weight of their overly muscled breasts and thighs. The lack of space in grower houses means that broilers sit in urine-saturated litter. Producers do not change or clean the litter during the chickens' six-week growing cycle. Consequently, the litter becomes increasingly wet and caked with urine and feces, resulting in burns and blisters on the breasts and the hocks, or the upper parts of the legs. These often require extensive treatment after rescue. Regardless of these obstacles, rescuers see the chickens as conscious individuals whose interests have been disregarded by the industrial farming system.

In contrast, poultry companies see the birds as commodities. Their response to a disaster is to do what is most economical, which often means bulldozing the facility, burying the birds, and starting over again. The corporate stories report losses of "product." The primary issue becomes one of carcass disposal. Rescue efforts mean bad publicity because, in learning about the disaster, the public also learns about the everyday conditions of factory farming. Poultry companies cite safety issues to keep rescuers and the public away from a site. As Coston explained about Buckeye's decision to end the rescue, "They cleared us out once they started getting press. That made them nervous. They were like, 'Stop. You have to stop. Back up and leave and we will deal with this ourselves.' So to them it was bad press. To us it was exposure." The growers and farm workers are often put in the middle during a rescue. The companies that breed, feed, and slaughter the animals own them, but the grower has the role, though temporary, of a steward. During Hurricane Katrina, one grower expressed concern over the birds' welfare, and workers were willing to handle the birds more humanely—at least in the presence of the rescuers. In the end, however, growers and workers were subject to the policies of the poultry companies.

I argue that the "solution" to disasters involving farmed animals does not involve rescuing as many as possible, although some rescue will occasionally have to take place. Rescue is a necessary and noble task, but the solution lies in another direction. It involves curtailing and eventually ending the perverse industrial farming practices that make animals so vulnerable. This is not a radical proposal. Intensive production methods, along with farm bills that favor large operations and federal subsidies for feed crops, have stoked Americans' appetites for animal products and kept meat, dairy, and egg prices low. But consumers have grown increasingly aware of and concerned for the welfare of animals and the quality of the food they eat. In one major survey, 79 percent said that farm animals have the right to be treated humanely.[27] In another survey, 68 percent agreed that the government should take an active role in promoting farm animal welfare, and 75 percent said they would support laws requiring farmers to treat animals more humanely.[28] Consumers have already influenced many producers to adopt more humane farming practices. Thus, the task for the management of disasters is to encourage measures that reduce animals' vulnerability without eliminating animal agriculture altogether. Recent reports from the Pew Commission on Industrial Farm Animal Production and the Union of Concerned Scientists (UCS) offer some concrete recommendations. Although their analyses did not specifically address disasters, the reports conclude that our current system of production harms not only animals but also public health and human communities. Consequently, the findings have practical implications for reducing the impact of disasters on animals and people.

In sum, both reports promote more sustainable animal agriculture, which is by definition safer for people and animals than our current methods. *Sustainability* is, of course, defined in human terms. For the animals who lose their lives, no agricultural practices are truly "sustainable." According to the Pew report, sustainability is "measured by the balance between agricultural inputs and outputs and ecosystem health, given the human population and rate of consumption."[29] Intensive practices are neither economically nor environmentally sustainable. They focus on producing more "units" through any means possible. In addition to the animal welfare implications, the environmental and public health risks of our current system are tremendous, even in normal times. The link between livestock and environmental problems, including climate change, has been well documented.[30] Making agricultural practices sustainable would reduce the harm to animals and people under all circumstances. The reports by the Pew Commission and the UCS reports make numerous recommendations in several areas. Here I focus on those having direct implications for disasters.

The Pew report recommends phasing out "the most intensive and inhumane production practices within a decade to reduce [Industrial Farm Animal Production] risks to public health and improve animal well-being."[31] These practices include veal crates for calves, gestation and farrowing crates for pigs, and battery cages for chickens. Indeed, Florida and Arizona have already banned veal and gestation crates, and several producers have agreed to phase out their use. Eliminating these practices would not take us back to "Old McDonald's farm"; but it does not mean that animals will be "free range." They will still be confined but will not be caged or tethered, and they will have greater freedom of movement. This step would greatly improve the odds for animals in a disaster. In particular, it raises the possibility of evacuation, or at least escape to what are known as "critter pads," elevated areas to which animals can move during flood. In Washington State, such areas have already saved cattle, chickens, and turkeys. To encourage the elimination of these "most intensive and inhumane" practices, the Pew Commission recommends that "the phase-out plan should include tax incentives, such as accelerated depreciation for new and remodeled structures, targeted to regional and family operations."[32] This simple step can make animals less vulnerable while not imposing costs on the people involved in implementing it.

The reports from both organizations discuss some of the better-researched housing alternatives, including hoop barns for hogs. A hoop barn is a semi-permanent structure with four-foot-high wood or concrete sidewalls fitted with a tubular arch, across which stretches a tarp made of opaque, ultraviolet-light-resistant polypropylene. Most of the floor space inside contains bedding of straw, cornstalks, or other crop residues. Part of the floor is a concrete slab where feeding and watering occurs. Hoop barns allow hogs to express their natural behaviors to burrow and root, and the open-ended construction provides natural ventilation, thus reducing the concentration of hydrogen sulfide, methane, and ammonia. The bedding absorbs waste, and it can be composted and used for fertilizer. In short, hoop barns provide a more humane environment for hogs, with far less toll on the environment. Production compares favorably with intensive housing systems.[33] Hoop barns have also been used successfully with beef and dairy cattle and poultry.

I mention hoop barns to illustrate one especially effective agricultural practice that can make animals less vulnerable in disasters. Pasture-based methods for raising cattle and hogs can even be applied to chickens, using easily moved structures. These methods would also make animals less vulnerable in disasters. However, they require more land, and production under these conditions might be more variable than it is under industrial conditions. Pasture-based methods would also increase the amount of labor involved in raising all animals and thus require more training in animal husbandry. Consequently, we need research that can help farmers incorporate profitable, sustainable practices. The UCS recommends research to determine the following:

- Which breeds will produce the best meat or eggs in different climates
- How many animals can be produced on pasture without compromising the environment or animal health

- What are the best pasture production systems for different climates
- How can animals be raised in pastures without using antibiotics
- What compounds can replace the current generation of growth promotants

To study these issues, the UCS and the Pew Commission call for reform in the funding of agricultural research. Currently, much of the research takes place at land-grant schools, through funding provided by agribusiness. Not surprisingly, the "solutions" to agricultural problems often involve products developed by companies that promote industrial farming practices. The Pew Commission recommends that funding from the federal government could reduce bias, so that research need not serve the interests of agribusiness.[34]

These recommendations for sustainable agriculture will seem at odds with my perspective on ending the exploitation of animals. Some animal advocates will dismiss my ideas as merely "welfarist." On a personal level, I believe that it is wrong to kill another living being—even if that being has lived a "good" life and suffers no pain in dying. I would love to bring readers around to my moral stance. At the same time, I realize that only about 3 percent of Americans are vegetarians. I also realize that millions of people worldwide rely on livestock for everything from food to livelihood to cultural identification.[35] I recognize the conditions that exist, and I want to improve the situation of animals within them. Consequently, I support any move to sustainable agriculture. However, the success of sustainability requires several concurrent developments. It depends on consumers who are willing to vote with their dollars. Thus, I support efforts to encourage those who will buy animal products anyway to purchase humanely raised products. Along with this, I would recommend implementing a reliable labeling program that can help people make purchases that are consistent with their moral commitment to reducing animal suffering. Currently, consumers have no access to accurate information about the conditions under which animals were raised. Consumers who want to make choices that are more humane are often misled by words such as "natural," which have nothing whatsoever to do with the treatment of animals. Although I do not know exactly what this program would look like, I can sketch out some components. It would differ from existing programs such as Certified Humane Raised and Handled and American Humane Certified. These voluntary programs enroll producers who raise their animals according to specific animal welfare standards. These programs are well intentioned, but they do not make farming practices visible to the consumer. For example, humane standards allow for the trimming of the beaks of egg-laying hens; they use the word *trimming* rather than *debeaking*. Although the two processes can differ, a consumer could easily think that "humanely" produced eggs come from hens who have not endured this practice at all. To make these and other practices visible to consumers, I support a system proposed by Jeff Leslie and Cass R. Sunstein, by which all animal products would carry a label informing consumers of the practices used in production. Thus, instead of having one shelf in the egg section of a supermarket designated for "cage free" eggs, all egg cartons would disclose the conditions in which the hens lived, using terms that consumers could easily understand. Consumers have the right to know that their meat, eggs, and dairy products came from animals who lived highly confined lives. As Leslie and Sunstein explain:

> A consumer-focused label might contain disclosure of the frequency with which chickens suffer from chemical burns caused by lying in unsanitary litter; . . . a label might disclose the frequency (or absence) of bruises, broken wings, and birds that are dead on arrival at the processing plant, all of which can result from rough handling. The label might also disclose the extent to which the producer provides the birds with access to straw, hay, or similar biodegradable material for environmental enrichment and expression of natural behaviors. The most effective label criteria are likely to be those that focus on health and welfare out-

comes for the animals that are not only important from an animal-welfare perspective but are also easily imagined by consumers.[36]

The details of course would differ by species. The system would require third-party verification. Many other details would have to be resolved. My larger point is that promoting sustainable farming requires making farming practices more visible so that people can make purchases consistent with their moral commitments. Under current conditions, people who choose to eat animal products and yet want to know the animals were not mistreated cannot consistently act on that commitment. Consumers need robust, reliable information about the choices available to them. A systematic labeling program can provide this information, and in turn, support sustainability, which can reduce the vulnerability of animals under all circumstances.

At the same time, I encourage those willing to consume fewer animal products to do so, for reasons that include reducing the impact on the environment and improving human health as well as compassion for animals. Many people would be more willing to make incremental changes, such as reducing the amount of meat they eat, than to stop eating meat altogether. Because the consumption of animal products is such a deeply entrenched practice, an incremental approach makes sense. To this end, I would like to see more meatless options in school and workplace cafeterias. Research by the Humane Research Council indicates that most Americans are unfamiliar with alternatives to meat and dairy products, but many would be willing to try them at no cost.[37] Here is an ideal opportunity for companies that produce soy and wheat meat substitutes and other such products to increase their visibility. I would also like to see plant-based foods become the default, so that people have to request meat or dairy options, rather than the other way around. Companies and school systems could promote plant-based foods one day a week and receive a financial incentive for making compassionate choices. Individual employees could also receive incentives, financial or otherwise, for choosing plant-based foods at lunch, much as homeowners can get tax credits for making houses more energy efficient. In short, we can take numerous steps to reduce the vulnerability of farmed animals. Under our existing system of production, the normal state of affairs is a disaster. Although some will argue that promoting sustainability is only excusing the inexcusable, within the context of disaster response, it will help animals as well as people.

At our current levels of consumption, factory farms are a necessary evil. If we intend to keep feeding a growing global population animal products at every meal, then, by necessity, we will need to confine animals to lives of suffering to satisfy our appetites. But if we reduce our appetites and use our shopping dollars to support sustainable practices, better lives are possible for animals—and for people. Fifty years ago, hurricanes and tornadoes did not mean the death of millions of chickens, hogs, and other animals. To be sure, animals lost their lives in natural disasters. They will always face some degree of risk. However, as the coverage of the Buckeye Farm rescue points out, the current system makes them "victims of a disaster caused—not by tornadoes—but by large-scale, intensive animal agriculture."[38] In factory farming, we have put the animals on whom we rely most heavily at a level of risk that would be unacceptable for any other living beings. During a disaster, they suffer needlessly. The producers incur significant losses. The environment undergoes irreversible damage. Rescuers endanger themselves saving animals whose quality of life is compromised from birth. The means to change this is within our reach. Alleviating the suffering of farm animals is not only a compassionate choice. In the context of disaster planning and response, it is also good public policy.

3 / Birds and Marine Wildlife

> I don't like to call it a disaster, because there has been no
> loss of human life. I am amazed at the publicity for the
> loss of a few birds.
>
> FRED HARTLEY, PRESIDENT OF UNION OIL COMPANY (1969)

Current concerns about oil and the environment express two dominant themes. One emphasizes the role of carbon-based fuels in climate change. The other emphasizes the hazards involved in drilling, especially in areas considered environmentally sensitive. In both instances animals are vulnerable, more so than humans. Because animals cannot escape the consequences of our petroleum addiction, they often face risks sooner and more directly. Yet, with the growing energy demands of the planet's human population, their vulnerability seems of little consequence. Why should the lives of a few birds matter, when we simply need more oil? When Fred Hartley spoke his mind about "a few birds" at a 1969 hearing of the Senate Subcommittee on Air and Water Pollution, he expressed a sentiment still held by some today.[1] Environmental policymakers continue to argue over whether a disaster that takes no human toll really constitutes a disaster.[2] This chapter takes oil spills as the focusing event for thinking about our responsibility to some of the wildest creatures on the planet. Moreover, because many spills involve human error or technological failure, in combination with forces of nature, they provide a contrast to the natural disasters discussed in the preceding chapters. No one is responsible for a hurricane or tornado, but when human error is involved, there is somewhere to place blame. Someone—most often a corporation—must finance the clean-up efforts. Often, however, this accountability introduces conflicts that only slow things down.

The incident that triggered Hartley's comment was the January 1969 blowout of a Union Oil drilling rig offshore from Santa Barbara, California. Efforts to cap an initial leak of natural gas caused a massive build-up of pressure. The pressure, in turn, pushed oil and gas up through five ruptures in the sea floor. Because the company lacked the tools and technology to control a spill of this size, it took workers eleven days to cap the well (although it leaked for months to come). Meanwhile, the oil had created an eight-hundred-square mile slick. Oil reportedly muted the sound of the waves as they washed ashore and polluted over thirty-five miles of coastline. Each wave carried the oil-coated carcasses of seals, dolphins, countless fish, and some four thousand seabirds. This figure dramatically underestimates the number of birds affected because of the inadequate techniques used to document bird mortality at the time.[3] The Santa Barbara Wildlife Care Network describes the rescue efforts:

> Volunteers were recruited to pluck oiled birds from local beaches. Grebes, cormorants and other seabirds were so sick, their feathers so soaked in oil that they were not difficult to catch. Birds were bathed in Polycomplex A-11, medicated, and placed under heat lamps to stave off pneumonia. The survival rate was less than 30 percent for birds that were treated. Many more died on the beaches where they had formerly sought their livelihoods. Those who had managed to avoid the oil were threatened by the detergents used to disperse the oil slick.[4]

Estimates collected by the National Research Council indicate that 380 million gallons of petroleum make their way from various sources into the world's oceans each year.[5] There are no precise data on the numbers of birds and animals affected by oil spills, but the annual figure is surely in the billions. The majority of catastrophic spills, and those that make the news, occur from groundings or collisions of ships that are either transporting oil or leak fuel oil because of damage.[6] A brief list of the high-profile spills illustrates the scope of the issue. In 1978, the *Amoco Cadiz* ran aground and split in two off the coast of Brittany. The tanker spilled 223,000 tons of heavy crude oil into the Atlantic Ocean. Rescuers recovered 20,000 dead birds; marine life in the area suffered tremendous mortality. The *Exxon Valdez* spill in 1989 killed an estimated quarter of a million birds, as well as countless sea otters, harbor seals, salmon, and creatures in the supporting food chain. In 1999, the tanker *Erika* broke in two and sank off the French coast, affecting an estimated 77,000 birds, most of whom did not survive. In 2000, the freighter *MV Treasure* sank off the coast of South Africa, contaminating over 20,000 African penguins, whose worldwide numbers are estimated at only 180,000. The rescue and rehabilitation effort was unprecedented in its size. It occurred just six years after the sinking of the tanker *Apollo Sea* in the same area contaminated 10,000 African penguins. In 2002, the sinking of the crude oil tanker *Prestige* off the coast of Spain and Portugal topped the *Exxon Valdez* as the worst spill and possibly the worst ecological disaster in history. As many as 300,000 sea birds died as a result.[7]

Accidents make the news and the images of blackened birds and spoiled coastlines cause public outrage. However, most petroleum pollution comes from "small but frequent" discharges of oil from various sources.[8] Some are land-based, such as the portion that comes from improperly disposed motor oil, highway run-off, and leakage from recreational boats. Others sources of oil are sea-based. A significant portion comes from standard shipping practices, such as loading or discharging at ports or the washing of tanks at sea. The industry considers these "operational spills" rather than accidents.[9] They seldom make the news, but they take a toll on birds and animals. For example, about forty-two thousand Magellanic penguins die annually just along one stretch of the coast of northern Argentina and southern Brazil, where shipping routes overlap with the penguins' migration route. The oil comes from the routine discharge of oil-contaminated ballast water and the washing of ships' tanks at sea. Researchers have documented this chronic oiling of penguins in the region for over thirty years, and it is one reason (along with overfishing) for concern about the conservation of the species.[10]

In some spills, the source of the oil remains unknown. A "mystery spill" off the coast of Santa Barbara in January 2005 harmed more birds than did the wreck of the *Prestige*.[11] A veterinarian who worked in both spills reported that the number of oiled birds picked up in three days during the Santa Barbara rescue exceeded the numbers found in three weeks in Spain. The oil could have come from naturally occurring oil seepage below the sea floor. Natural seepage accounts for more than half of the oil in North American waters, or about forty-seven 47 million gallons a day.[12] Seeps regularly trap and contaminate countless birds and marine mammals. In some regions, such as coastal southern California, natural seepages account for the equivalent of a "massive year-round oil spill."[13]

Oil spills are a dramatic and very visible form of ocean pollution. Images of water, beaches and birds smeared with thick, black oil invoke the need to define victims and villains, as well as the desire to help. In the 1969 Senate subcommittee hearing, Hartley explained the Santa Barbara event as a "blow up of the earth's crust" and blamed "Mother Nature" for "letting the oil come out."[14] The American public, Congress, and scores of researchers thought otherwise. Environmentalists blamed intentional short cuts and policies that favored the oil company. Although the event was accidental, circumstances set the stage for it to happen. The U.S. Geological Survey had allowed Union Oil to use shorter protective casings than federal standards typically required. The state of California had even stricter standards than those set by the federal government, but the rig stood more than three miles offshore, outside California's jurisdiction. The event made a growing number of people aware of environmental issues and galvanized grassroots efforts that had been sparked by the 1962 publication of Rachel Carson's *Silent Spring*. In the year following the spill, President Richard Nixon signed the National Environmental Policy Act, requiring federal agencies to assess the impact of major projects, such as oil exploration on public lands, and established the Environmental Protection Agency.[15] On April 22, 1970, Americans across the country participated in the first Earth Day.[16]

Oil spills have always generated questions of responsibility and appropriate response. Hartley's remark, depicting disasters only in human terms, epitomizes one position. This view stands against the position that no event affects only the other beings on this planet, leaving humans unscathed and untroubled. In this view, as we humans strove to bring ever-increasing parts of the environment under our control, we subjected animals to increased vulnerability. For example, successful agriculture involves eliminating animals labeled "pests" and "vermin." Our efforts to control insect populations with the pesticide DDT nearly produced the "silent spring" Carson predicted because the chemical thinned the shells of birds' eggs, resulting in high mortality among some species. In another instance, the expansion of suburbs into wildlands has eliminated habitat and increased the number of conflicts between humans and wildlife, creating a game that animals always lose, usually at the end of a gun. The examples abound. Because we have extended our reach into wilderness, polar regions, rainforests, and oceans, as expressed by Adrian Franklin, "no animals are safe and their only hope of survival lies with the willingness of humans to take moral responsibility for their protection."[17] In taking responsibility for animals and birds, we have raised new moral and practical questions about the consequences of our efforts to repair the damage.

Our Long Love Affair with Oil

With the exception of natural seeps, humans are responsible for all the oil in the marine environment. We have a long relationship with petroleum, and it has rather quickly become indispensable in nearly every aspect of daily life in industrial societies.

Petroleum is a Latin word meaning "rock" and "oil," and ancient peoples found various uses for the sticky substance that oozed out in natural seepages. The story of Noah's Ark mentions that he water-proofed the vessel using "pitch," or very thick petroleum that is essentially natural asphalt. For much of history, people used petroleum only rarely as fuel but more often as a medicinal substance, particularly for topical application to treat skin diseases. Coal provided the fuel for the Industrial Revolution, and our needs for energy have increased steadily since then. In the mid-1800s, innovations in fuel lamps drove the demand for lamp oils. In response, geologists produced the first kerosene, which is a colorless liquid fuel distilled from petroleum.[18] Its popularity inspired the drilling of wells to bring oil to the surface. The ensuing search for more oil led to an international industry.

What comes out of the ground is crude oil. Its chemical structure consists of hydrocarbon chains that can be separated through distillation. The resulting products include gasoline, jet and diesel fuel, liquid petroleum gas, kerosene, and several fuel oils. The addition of additives can produce asphalt, lubricants (such as motor oil), waxes, sulfuric acid, and olefins (which become plastics of various sorts). For crude oil to be turned into more useful products, it must move from wells to refineries. Initially, refineries were located close to oil fields. As refining became more sophisticated, issues of safety and profitability led oil companies to locate their refineries closer to markets. The crude oil was moved through pipelines and, for longer distances, shipped in barrels. The first tanker ship, the *Glückauf*, carried oil in bulk from the United States to Europe in 1886. The innovation dramatically reduced the cost of transporting oil. Today, thousands of tanker ships currently ply the seas.[19]

Oil tankers vary widely in capacity, but the trend has been toward ever-larger ships. Two factors prompted the tanker industry to build larger vessels and to enlarge or "jumboize" many ships within the existing fleet: the western world's increasing appetite for oil and the closures of the Suez Canal from 1956 to 1957 and from 1967 to 1975. The canal has had a vital role in the transportation of oil since its opening in the nineteenth century.[20] It greatly shortened the voyage from the Middle East to Europe, but its depth and width limited the size of the tankers it could accommodate. When the canal closed, tankers had to take the longer—and less profitable—route around South Africa. No longer constrained by the canal, tanker operators made the trip worthwhile by transporting oil in increasingly larger ships.[21] During the 1950s, the tanker classification system had only three categories of vessels, reflecting the size of the world's carrier fleet at the time. Beginning in the late 1960s, the previously "large range" was renamed "large range 1" to accommodate the "large range 2." Then even larger vessels were built, the "very large crude carrier," which carries two million barrels, and the "ultra large crude carrier," which carries three million.[22] These two carriers, which are used primarily to transport crude oil, are nicknamed "supertankers."[23] They are the largest commercial vessels ever built. Refined petroleum products, such as gasoline, are typically transported in small or medium-sized carriers. All of these vessels are susceptible to accidents, but the supertankers have caused the most catastrophic spills and the greatest environmental damage in history.

Supertankers transport oil very efficiently, but at considerable risk. Their size makes them difficult to maneuver. They take miles and miles to come to a stop. Stopping distance becomes a particular problem near coastlines, where the vessels are especially vulnerable to accidents. The first major tanker spill occurred in March 1967, when the *Torrey Canyon,* one of the first of the supertankers, went aground on a granite reef off the southwest coast of England. Built in 1959 to carry a cargo of sixty thousand tons, the *Torrey Canyon* underwent "jumboization" in 1964 to carry twice that much. On its fateful voyage in March 1967, it held a full cargo of crude oil from Kuwait bound for Wales. Over thirty million gallons spilled out when it ran aground, resulting in an enormous slick that contaminated hundreds of miles of Cornish and French coastline. Edward Cowan, leading scholar of the incident, points out that if a tanker had run aground in the same area twenty years earlier, the resulting spill would have amounted to only one-fifth of what the *Torrey Canyon* lost. The spill would have been a local crisis rather than an international one. Such was the pace of technology.[24]

The incident brought global attention to a new hazard: major oil spills at sea. As one observer wrote, "The *Torrey Canyon* disaster revealed ignorance. Man had figured out how to move enormous quantities of oil but not how to cope when the system fails on a grand scale."[25] According to another, the people of England and France "reacted to the menace with fear, rage and wonder."[26] Every aspect brought lessons for a world unprepared for a disaster of this kind. Existing techniques for oil spill response were ineffective in such a massive incident.

Every oil spill, like every hurricane or earthquake, is unique. Each one involves different factors of setting, weather, type of oil, population, and severity of damage to the ship. Nevertheless, the response strategies used in similar types of disasters are the same. For oil spills, the response is most effective if it begins very quickly, while the oil is still on the water rather than on the beach and before the waves begin to break up the larger slicks. Techniques used to collect oil on the water's surface include containing the oil with mechanical booms and skimming up as much as possible. Other common techniques include burning and spreading chemical dispersants that "act like liquid soap to break up surface oil slicks into tiny droplets that must then be driven by wind and wave action into the water columns and diluted with huge volumes of water." Dispersants have been called "the oilmen's way of solving pollution by dilution . . . out of sight, out of mind."[27] Although the surface looks clean, the droplets of oil remain highly toxic. Moreover, the dispersants themselves are hazardous chemicals.

In the case of the *Torrey Canyon*, rough seas foiled the plan to contain the oil using an enormous plastic boom. In Britain, the response involved the repeated use of excessively large amounts of dispersants. It was not known at the time that the dispersants were themselves highly toxic and would cause extensive environmental damage of their own. The British government also tried burning the slick and finally resorted to bombing the site to reduce the amount of oil that would leak out over the course of years. The French had better results using straw and sawdust, rather than chemicals. However, the French faced the obstacle of having no state support for the response. The scale of the incident triggered the implementation of the national response plan intended for post-nuclear disaster, in which communities would be cut off from one another. It assumed that localities would take full responsibility for any response efforts. However, officials in Brittany had no expertise for such an incident, and the lack of support from Paris initially caused chaos and anger.

The *Torrey Canyon* spill prompted international legislation on oil pollution, which was woefully inadequate at the time.[28] Whereas oil spill management had been unprepared for the inevitability of large-scale spills, wildlife rescue was virtually an unknown terrain. The coasts of Cornwall and Brittany provide a nesting area for several species of sea birds, including puffins, guillemots, and razorbills. The spill occurred during the birds' annual northerly migration from North Africa, Spain, and southern France to the British Isles. Typically, the birds arrive exhausted after a flight of several hundred miles. Once on the coast of Cornwall, they feast on the rich bounty of the sea. This time, however,

> those birds that touched down on oil-covered waters, or were washed over by the advancing black tide, and subsequently made it to shore, were in pitiful shape. Their feathers were clotted and scraggly. Their throats and intestines had been seared by oil or detergent. Postmortems were to find lungs clogged with froth. Most had been profoundly chilled by the disruptive effect of the oil on their bodies' natural insulation. Many could not fly because of shock and exhaustion. Among those rescued and cared for, an acute loss of appetite was noted. The birds could not assist in their own recoveries by taking proper nourishment. Few survived.[29]

The local bird hospital normally treated a few hundred birds a year, but it saw 4,000 just in the week following the wreck. The Royal

Society for the Prevention of Cruelty to Animals set up additional emergency cleaning stations in the area, but the efforts were mostly in vain. Of the 7,849 birds rescued, only 450 remained alive by mid-April, and most of these died soon after that. Less than 1 percent survived long enough to be released. Estimates on the total number of birds killed range from 30,000 to 75,000. They died from the oil and the dispersants used to break it up but also from improper handling and from exposure to the harsh, solvent-based cleaners in use at the time. Marine species such as limpets, barnacles, and shellfish also suffered widespread mortality and a rare species of hermit crab has disappeared from the area since the spill.[30]

What Does Oil Do to Birds and Mammals?

Oil causes suffering to birds and mammals through ingestion and physical contact, most often in combination. Birds stay warm and waterproof through the complex arrangement of their feathers like shingles on a roof.[31] Each feather consists of a stiff but hollow central shaft that runs its entire length. Vanes extend to each side of the shaft, and a system of barbs makes up the vane. The barbs have microscopic hook-and-loop structures, called barbicels, that keep the feather together. When a feather is out of place, only birds know how to repair it through preening. The urge to preen overrides all other instincts, including the need to eat and drink.

The structure of plumage creates a wind- and waterproof barrier that helps the bird stay afloat. Even a tiny amount of oil can compromise a bird's ability to remain insulated and waterproof.[32] Oil-soaked feathers cannot trap air to keep the bird warm, putting the bird at risk for hypothermia. The feathers mat together and lose their ability to provide waterproofing. Moreover, the birds try to remove the oil and restore the integrity of the feathers by preening. Through preening they ingest oil, which causes extensive internal damage. Oil-soaked birds attempt to get warm by seeking shelter on land, where they become vulnerable to predators or die from malnutrition and dehydration. They can also be poisoned by eating oil-contaminated vegetation or prey.

Marine mammals too face many potential risks from petroleum. They spend much of their time at the water's surface, making it more likely that they will be exposed to oil slicks. The heavy fur coats of sea otters function much as feathers do for birds by keeping them warm and buoyant. Unlike other marine mammals, which have the protection of a layer of blubber, sea otters rely entirely on their fur for insulation. The fur traps a layer of air next to the animal's skin that keeps cold water away from the skin. Otters groom themselves continually to maintain the integrity of their coats. The combination of thick fur, which readily retains oil, and the drive to groom, which causes them to ingest oil, makes otters extremely vulnerable in spills. When oil-soaked, the fur cannot maintain the air layer, and the result is hypothermia. Mammals without haircoats, including dolphins and whales, some species of seals, and sea lions, do not face the same risk of hypothermia because, with the exception of juvenile animals, their blubber protects them from the cold. Nevertheless, these animals face risks from inhalation, skin exposure, and ingestion of oil. For example, following the Santa Barbara spill, oil clogged the blowholes of dolphins, causing lung hemorrhages.[33] Following the *Exxon Valdez* spill, according to petroleum industry reports, gray and harbor seals suffered from "respiratory distress . . . conjunctivitis, corneal ulcers, skin ulceration and bleeding of the gastro-intestinal tract and lungs."[34] Like birds, marine mammals also face risks from ingesting oil-contaminated prey and vegetation.

The process of cleaning birds and animals has been described as "relatively expensive and logistically complicated."[35] It involves far more than simply cleaning off the oil. If you have ever walked along a beach and stepped in a blob of "tar," which is oxidized crude oil, you know how hard it is to remove, even from the relatively durable human skin of the feet. I lived in South Florida for nearly two decades, where lifeguard stands along the beaches provide turpentine or mineral spirits and rags to remove tar from the feet of beachgoers. These solvents suffice for small amounts of oil on the tough skin on one's heel. However, when solvent-based products were used for cleaning contaminated birds, mortality rates and side effects were high. The human rescuers also faced risks. In incidents before the 1970s, rehabilitators reported suffering rashes and headaches from exposure to solvents.[36] It would take another disaster before methods were found to rescue birds and animals safely.

The Standard Oil Disaster

In February 1971, two Standard Oil tankers collided under the Golden Gate Bridge in San Francisco, spilling nearly one million gallons of bunker oil, the fuel oil used on ships.[37] The oil fouled over fifty miles of California coastline. Volunteers rescued approximately six thousand oiled birds, but the spill affected as many as twenty thousand. Those who worked in the rescue effort knew relatively little about the rehabilitation of birds at the time, but that soon changed.[38]

The Standard Oil spill effectively signaled the start of seabird rehabilitation in the United States and the genesis of a leading organization dedicated to the task. It began when Alice Berkner, a registered nurse, accompanied a veterinarian friend to one of the numerous sites that had been set up in the spill area to treat oiled birds. She describes the experience of entering the treatment center:

> As long as I live I will never forget the odor that assaulted me as I walked through the doors of the Center. It was a horrendous mix of rotting fish, bird droppings, oil, and, strangely enough, vitamin B. Almost as bad was the noise! I've been sensitive to loud noise all my life and the nightmarish mix of screaming birds, guitar music, fork lifts, and people voicing the complete range of human emotions in that echo chamber of a building threatened to deafen me. I was not two feet through the door when a woman came rushing toward the exit, tears streaming down her face, wailing "I've been here twenty-four hours and they won't give me my own bird!" It got worse, much worse.[39]

Berkner questioned the treatment of the birds at the time, which involved measures such as giving them bread and milk, foods that birds would never consume naturally, and "medication combinations that would have killed people." It was, she says, "a new field with no history or guidelines of care or treatment."[40] Because of her nursing background, she had experience in triage and saw the pitfalls in the existing system.

Although Standard Oil was partially funding the rescue effort, most of the equipment and supplies were donated. Volunteers provided labor. The Berkeley Ecology Center initially served as a conduit for funding, but after officials from Standard Oil argued in favor of establishing a separate, nonprofit bird care organization, in April 1971, the International Bird Rescue and Research Center (IBRRC) was founded. The new organization, which the founders still refer to as "Bird Rescue," moved into space donated by the Berkeley Humane Society. The group had to house the birds until September, when they would molt their ruined feathers. Meanwhile, Berkner and others found a niche for themselves. "When the last birds were released," Berkner says, "the few of us that remained decided to continue the organization."

The founding members were pleased with the number of birds they had saved but not satisfied with the results. They educated themselves about the work to which they had dedicated themselves. Berkner recalls, "One of the first and I feel, most valuable things we did was to institute a literature search in the area of seabirds, their anatomy and physiology, how they were affected by oil, the use of medication in aviculture and anything remotely connected to the problems we had experienced." When oiled birds arrive at rescue centers, they are usually highly stressed and exhausted. They may suffer from hypothermia or have broken bones and other injuries. The longer they have been exposed to oil, the poorer their chances for survival. As researchers report,

Experience has shown that the amount of wildlife contamination is not the primary determinant of survivability, but how long the animal has been exposed. A highly oiled bird that has been captured and stabilized within a few hours of being contaminated has a greater chance of survival, and will undergo less suffering than a lightly oiled one left in the wild for days.[41]

Before cleaning, rescuers first make certain the birds are stable enough to go through the procedure. Stabilization can take as long as forty-eight hours, during which the birds receive fluids and are kept warm and quiet. Rescuers flush oil from the birds' eyes and gastrointestinal tract. Medication such as activated charcoal can prevent additional oil from being absorbed in the digestive system.

Once the birds are stable, the cleaning can begin. It took trial-and-error to find just the right product for the job. Berkner describes the process: "We actively investigated the use of solvent to clean oiled birds but were very concerned with the toxicity factors involved with its use. It was during our four years at the Humane Society site that we read of detergent cleaning techniques developed in England." Berkner and others tested dozens of products on oil-coated feathers and found that Dawn detergent cleaned the birds without introducing additional toxins. Dawn has proven to be the most effective substance in removing oil from plumage without harming the skin of the birds or animals, the people treating them, or the environment.[42] Today, stabilized birds undergo thorough baths in a 1 percent solution of Dawn. The process, according to IBRRC,

requires two people; one keeps the bird submerged in the tub and controls the bird's head. The other person agitates the soapy water through the bird's feathers and cleans its head and neck using tooth brushes, q-tips and Waterpiks®. The bird is moved to new tubs of soapy water until the water in the tub is clear and no oil remains. This process can take from 10 minutes to an hour depending on the size of bird or amount of oil that has to be removed.[43]

Not only must birds be free of oil and other contaminants, they also must have no traces of detergent on their skin or plumage. Washed birds are placed in warm air dryers, then in warm water, followed by cool water. Rescuers monitor them closely during the recovery process. Before release, the birds must demonstrate that they have regained their waterproofing by staying afloat. Their feathers must be able to keep moisture away from their bodies. After passing this test, birds are banded (in the United States, by the Fish and Wildlife Service) and released. Where the habitat remains contaminated, birds and animals must be relocated before release.

One of the challenges facing wildlife rescue organizations is to bring the plight of animals to public awareness without prompting the involvement of untrained but well-intentioned citizen rescuers. Birds and animals are the most innocent victims of an oil spill. However, they are usually wary of humans, and handling can add stress to injuries already suffered. Moreover, because birds and other wildlife must eventually be released, improper handling can have a negative effect on their ability to return to their environment. In the United States, state and federal laws protect wildlife species. Wildlife rehabilitators hold state and federal permits (through the U.S. Fish and Wildlife Service) and many have local certification, too.

Media images of blackened birds and animals, dead and dying along an oil-fouled shore, drive public support for rescue activities. This support would intensify during the *Exxon Valdez* incident, when the sea otter emerged as media star and metaphor. However, media coverage and public support had the unintended consequence of making otters more vulnerable by impeding the very activities they sought to encourage.

The *Exxon Valdez*

Just after midnight on March 24, 1989, the tanker *Exxon Valdez* struck a reef in Prince William Sound, Alaska, spilling more than 11 million gallons of crude oil, equal to 257,000 barrels. Lacking a reference point to visualize such volume, I went searching for an equivalent, but even picturing 125 Olympic-size swimming pools is out of my range. This was the largest spill in U.S. history.[44] The exact reasons for the grounding remain unclear. The tanker had encountered icebergs in the shipping lanes and Captain Joe Hazelwood had ordered the helmsman, Harry Claar, to take the vessel out of the shipping lanes until it was clear of the ice. Claar turned the helm over to Robert Kagan and left the third mate, Gregory Cousins, in charge of the wheelhouse. Cousins and Kagan did not make the turn back into the shipping lanes and instead ran aground on Bligh Reef. Investigations by the National Transportation Safety Board determined five probable causes, including improper maneuvering by the third mate because of fatigue, possibly combined with alcohol impairment, and failure by the Coast Guard to provide an effective traffic system.[45] The captain was charged with operating a vessel while under the influence of alcohol, but an Alaska jury found him not guilty.

A series of delays slowed the cleanup after the *Exxon Valdez* spill. Mechanical skimmers were not immediately available. During the first application of dispersants, the water was too calm to mix the chemical with the oil, a requirement for effective use. Although a trial burn in an isolated area proved successful, a storm on the third day made additional burning and thus all efforts to contain the oil at sea impossible. Consequently, cleanup efforts shifted from the water to the shoreline.

As the oil dissolved and spread underwater, it killed millions of fish, including pink salmon and Pacific herring, as well as the countless creatures in the supporting food chain and the coastal ecology. The area had two orca pods, one of which lost half of its members and the other a third. No new calves were born for at least four years after the spill. The spill was particularly devastating to birds. Prince William Sound is known for its "rich and diverse" marine bird populations. Its bays and inland seas include habitat ranging from rugged islands to rocky outcrops, from coastal forests to sandy shoreline. Two hundred species of birds use the sound at various times during the year. Estimates suggest the spill killed at least a quarter of a million birds. The oil, however, was not the only culprit; the detergents, dispersants, and high-pressure hot water used in the clean-up of the shoreline killed by weight as many animals as did the initial oiling.[46]

Sea otters, especially breeding females and their pups, suffered high mortality because of the spill. Between thirty-five hundred and fifty-five hundred otters were estimated to have died from exposure to oil, out of a population of ten thousand in the entire oiled area. No response plan for sea otters was in place at the time of the spill, and a week elapsed before the deployment of the first rescue vessels. For these creatures, as for birds exposed to oil, time is of the essence. Many otters captured within the first week of rescue had already been heavily oiled for several days, and survival rates were low.[47]

Before the spill, according to one account, otters "swam peacefully in the coastal waters of southern Alaska, enjoying little recognition from the general public."[48] But immediately following the spill, when the childlike, playful mammals appeared in the media "rubbing their eyes and grooming their fur in a futile attempt to rid their coats of the slimy crude oil," they quickly captured public attention.[49] The sea otter became the "poster child" of the incident. Although the spill affected far more birds than it did sea otters, the anthropomorphic otters became the perfect victims of the disaster. The otters put an adorable, furry face on the effects of the oil.

When press accounts of the spill revealed that it would significantly affect wildlife, the story quickly became one of international interest. A LexisNexis search using the terms *sea otters* and *oil* reveals 249 articles in the U.S. and world media during the twelve months following March 24, 1989, compared with only 23 articles in the preceding year. The U.S. Fish and Wildlife Service, the agency charged with the management of sea otters in Alaska (under the Marine Mammal Protection Act), usually receives 140 queries a year at its Anchorage office on all topics related to its activities. In the six months following the spill, the service received more than 460 press queries just on otters, representing a 600 percent increase. The media exploited the appeal of the otters, often portraying them as being at the mercy of a bureaucratic tangle that was preventing their rescue. In response to stories with headlines such as, "U.S. Bureaucracy Halts the Rescuers of Sea Otters," and "Rescuing Animals Difficult: Scores of Otters Likely to Perish," the public swamped the Fish and Wildlife Service and the Department of Interior with letters and telephone calls demanding the dedication of all available resources to the task of saving otters. The press's combination of "sea otter-as-symbol" with "sea otter-as-victim," according to one report, "resulted in the involvement of an emotional public in virtually every aspect of sea otter activities." The Fish and Wildlife Service was accustomed to acting within "the rational environment of a hermetically sealed science community."[50] Now, each action was delayed, probed, and challenged, first by the press and then by a hostile public. Staff members had to divert precious time from their rescue-related activities to conduct interviews. In sum, the interest generated among the media and the public by the "teddy bears" of the sea significantly slowed rescue efforts and related decisions.

Weighing the Costs of Rescue and Rehabilitation

The sea otter publicity following the *Exxon Valdez* spill demonstrates that the public will demand action, even when those responsible for that action are still considering what to do. Media images of birds and wildlife being cleaned and cared for reassure the public that something positive is being done. Recent research suggests, however, that the costs of rehabilitation might not always pay off. One study examined seabirds who were rescued, cleaned, and released after spills occurring between 1969 and 1994. On average, only 35 percent of the birds brought to rescue centers survived to be released.[51] Eighty to 90 percent of rehabilitated birds died within ten days of release, including many that had been determined to be healthy at the time (i.e., they were of healthy weight, with normal blood chemistry and plumage). In a control group, non-oiled birds of the same species had a life expectancy of a year and a half. Another study tracked brown pelicans who were rescued and cleaned after one of two southern California spills in 1990 and

1991. The birds had been fitted with radio transmitters during reha-bilitation. Two years later, researchers could account for only 10 percent of the rehabilitated pelicans, compared with 55 percent of those in a control group, forcing the authors to conclude that "cur-rent rehabilitation techniques are not effective in returning healthy birds to the wild."[52] Studies in Britain and the Netherlands report that fewer than 20 percent of rehabilitated birds survived their first year, and in one case, less than 1 percent did so.[53] A study assessing the outcome of sea otter rehabilitation efforts following the *Exxon Valdez* spill determined that the cost of capture and rehabilitation was $18.3 million, or $80,000 per animal.[54]

Survival rates and costs raise the question, When the next spill occurs, what should we do for the birds and animals? Should they be put through the stress of capture and treatment, only to die soon afterward? Despite the poor survival rates in the studies cited here, a strong argument can be made for continued rescue activity. Cap-turing oiled birds and wildlife and retrieving carcasses makes sense on several levels. First, it is an animal welfare issue, and the pub-lic demands a response. As conveyed in a statement by the IBRRC, "The public will not stand for wildlife agencies euthanizing oiled birds as they come ashore."[55] Second, retrieving oiled wildlife or carcasses reduces potential secondary impacts, such as ingestion by birds and animals who scavenge oiled carcasses. Third, capture and carcass retrieval can also be a public safety measure, because it min-imizes the possibility of contact between humans and oiled—and possibly ill or injured—wildlife. When wildlife specialists handle oiled birds and wildlife, the public at-large is less likely to inter-vene, even when unqualified to do so. Finally, arguments against rehabilitating oiled wildlife pose a false dichotomy of irreconcilable positions: we either do or do not engage in rehabilitation. There is a middle ground. Rather than rehabilitate every oiled bird, reha-bilitators can—and many do—ask a series of questions about the health of the individual and about the prospects of the species. Spe-cies that are threatened or endangered or whose loss would have an adverse affect on the population within a region would merit reha-bilitation. Those with abundant numbers would not.

Questions about whether to rehabilitate, however, skirt the issue of reducing vulnerability. One suggestion for doing so, and perhaps the most obvious one, involves reducing our use of oil through conservation and the development of alternative fuel sources. Unfortunately, our best efforts will not free us entirely from the need for oil. Even renewable energy does not offer the solution. Experts predict that renewable sources will supply less than 10 percent of our energy requirements over the next thirty years.[56] Meanwhile, global energy demand will continue to rise. Fossil fuels will continue to meet most of our energy needs because they are simply more economical and easier to store and transport. Moreover, even if we somehow stopped using petroleum, natural seeps would still leak oil into the marine environment.

Although we cannot evacuate birds and wildlife, there are ways to keep them away from oil. Research has demonstrated experimental success with systems that deter birds from landing on or swimming in oiled areas. The deterrence system uses sound, light, or motion to scare the birds away, functioning essentially as an "automated scarecrow."[57] After an initial period of success, however, birds become habituated to the deterrent. In response, researchers have experimented with radar-activated systems, which activate the deterrent only when birds are present. These have not yet been used in an actual oil spill, and although they would be costly to implement, such systems could save countless birds, as well as the money and labor required for rescue. Unfortunately, there are no deterrents yet available for diving birds, who are usually the most heavily oiled victims of spills.

Policy and legislation are certainly a large part of the solution. Each oil spill has brought new regulations intended to minimize the potential damage in the future. Predictably, each set of regulations has an attendant set of loopholes. For example, the *Torrey Canyon* incident prompted the International Maritime Organization to convene the International Convention for the Prevention of Pollution from Ships.[58] The resulting treaties regulate the operational and accidental discharge of oil at sea and provide sanctions for violation. However, through the system of "open registry," also called "flags of necessity" or, less neutrally, "flags of convenience," vessel owners can legally circumvent the rules. Briefly, the flag that a ship flies designates the laws that apply to it. A vessel owner can register a ship through a "phantom" company, even one existing only out of a filing cabinet, in a country whose regulations are favorable or profitable. Proponents argue that open registry is the only way ship owners operate profitably. Owners in one country can gain access to finance in another and a crew in yet another. Environmentalists and maritime labor organizations counter that flags of convenience allow shippers to avoid taxes, hire non-union crews, and skirt environmental regulations. Although not all shippers who use flags of convenience intend to engage in corrupt practices, the system nevertheless "enables less scrupulous operators to register their ships under flags which they know will not require full compliance with international rules."[59]

Open registry has significant implications for oil spill prevention, accountability, and compensation. The 2002 case of the aging tanker *Prestige* offers a good example. The vessel broke in half in severe weather and caused Spain's worst environmental disaster. It was carrying about twenty million gallons of fuel oil, which is a heavy blend gathered from the bottom of tanks after refining. Fuel oil is highly toxic and viscous, making it both hazardous and extremely difficult to clean up. The vessel itself was registered in the Bahamas but owned by a Greek family allegedly operating through a company based in Liberia. The petroleum cargo of the *Prestige* belonged to a Russian company based in Switzerland but operating through a British agent. The ship had a Filipino crew. The estimated impact of the spill in Spain, Portugal, and France is $900 million. The owners of the *Prestige* carried the minimal $25 million insurance for clean-up costs, and international maritime law caps the owner's responsibility at $80 million. The International Oil Pollution Compensation Funds, which provide assistance through fines levied on the oil industry, had only $186 million available. Although the captain and officers of the *Prestige* were arrested, the owners and the oil company went unpunished. The issue of accountability raised numerous moral and logistical questions. One journalist framed them aptly: "Whom," he asks, "does a Galician fisherman call about compensation for his threatened livelihood? And how much longer must a world revolted by spills put up with these daisy chains of responsibility?"[60]

The *Prestige* incident is especially tragic in the light of a set of regulations that were already in place to eliminate substandard vessels. These regulations require new petroleum tankers to have double hulls and require shipping companies to retire or retrofit their oldest and largest single-hulled vessels first. With a double hull, a collision only floods the ship's bottom compartment. Double hulls can significantly reduce the amount of spillage in grounding accidents; estimates say that the *Exxon Valdez* spill would have been 60 percent smaller if the ship had had a double hull. Double hulls have been required in passenger vessels for several decades. The United States introduced the mandate for oil tankers calling at U.S. ports as part of the Oil Pollution Act of 1990, and all tankers in U.S. waters must have double hulls by 2015.[61] The International Maritime Organization and the European Commission had introduced double-hull legislation for vessels in European waters in 1992. When the single-hulled tanker *Erika* sank and oiled the coast of Brittany in 1999, the two organizations sped up the phase-out deadlines for such vessels. The twenty-six-year-old, single-hulled *Prestige* would have been banned in European waters by 2005.

Although all experts agree that double hulls can significantly reduce the damage from tanker spills, oil companies have presented obstacles and found loopholes in the regulations. For example, Congress had attempted to introduce double-hull requirements and other measures to reduce oil pollution fifteen years before the *Exxon Valdez* spill. Opponents in the oil and shipping industry argued that the double-hull mandates "disrupt oil transportation and potentially affect the national economy."[62] To be sure, the expense of replacing a single-hulled ship is significant. A new, double-hulled tanker built in the United States can cost $300 million. To save money, some tanker owners do not replace their retiring single-hulled tankers with double-hulled ships. Instead, they simply replace them with younger single-hulled vessels.[63] Purportedly, some oil and tanker companies plan to continue to use single-hulled tankers until the 2015 phase-out deadline, which is also the anticipated date of the depletion of the Alaska oilfields. There is some question, however, whether U.S. shipyards can build enough new tankers to replace the single-hulled fleet by the deadline, when more ships will be in demand, especially if vessel operators hedge their bets by delaying placing their orders.[64]

B ecause we all use oil and other petroleum products, we all share the blame for making birds and marine animals vulnerable to oil spills. It is easy to point at the oil companies. But they are merely extracting and delivering a product we all demand in greater amounts, and at prices we deem affordable. Accidental spills will inevitably occur, and some of these will be on a major scale. In a spill, we face a moral imperative to remedy the damage for which we are responsible. How to remedy the damage without causing more—intentionally or otherwise—is the next big question.

We make birds and animals vulnerable by moving petroleum across the globe. The least we can do is ensure that our efforts to save them do not also put them at risk.

4 / Animals in Research Facilities

Prayer of the Mouse
I am so little and grey, dear God, how can You keep me
in mind? Always spied upon, always chased. Nobody ever
gives me anything, and I nibble meagrely at life. Why do
they reproach me with being a mouse? Who made me but
You? I only ask to stay hidden.

CARMEN BERNOS DE GASZTOLD, *PRAYERS FROM THE ARK* (1969)

Although most Americans know that large numbers of dogs and cats died after Hurricane Katrina, few know that 8,000 animals at Louisiana State University's Health Sciences Center School of Medicine met the same fate. The animals discussed in this chapter received virtually no media attention. Those who did not drown during the flood or starve in the weeks following it were euthanized. In 1992, after Hurricane Andrew, several hundred animals escaped from research facilities at the University of Miami. Although the animals had been used in AIDS research, they were "disease-free and harmless if left alone."[1] Alarmed by rumors that the animals carried HIV, area residents fatally shot 211 of them. At a nearby commercial breeding facility, 2,500 animals escaped when Andrew flattened gates and fences. Handlers said most of the animals could not survive on their own.

In addition to these deaths from what we call "natural" disasters, animals in research facilities suffer and die in human-caused or "man-made" disasters, such as accidents and technological failures. In human terms, the threshold for qualifying as a man-made disaster is twenty deaths or fifty injured.[2] Yet, human error or technological failure routinely results in animal deaths in numbers far exceeding this threshold, with little fanfare or public outcry. For example, a failed generator caused a power outage in July 2006 on the medical campus of Ohio State University. When electricity was restored, it triggered the heating system and temperatures soared to 105 degrees. Nearly 700 animals died. In 2005, failure of a ventilation unit at Wyeth Pharmaceuticals in Collegeville, Pennsylvania, caused hundreds of animals to die or to suffer such distress that they had to be euthanized. When reporters from the *Philadelphia Inquirer* followed up on the incident, they were told that the number of deaths was "not unusual." In 1988, workers at a National Institutes of Health (NIH) facility in Bethesda, Maryland, failed to restore electrical power to a building after performing maintenance on the heating, air conditioning, and alarm systems. The lack of fresh air killed 130 animals.[3]

I have been vague about the species and described the victims simply as "animals" for a purpose. Knowing the species changes the scenario and highlights the importance of the social construction of animals in our moral considerations. The 211 escaped animals who were shot by South Florida residents were rhesus monkeys. The animals who escaped from the breeding facility were monkeys and baboons. Those who suffocated at the National Institutes of Health facility and Wyeth Pharmaceuticals were mice. Of the 8,000 animals who died at Louisiana State University (LSU) following Katrina, some were dogs and monkeys but mice and rats made up the majority. Of those who died at Ohio State University, nearly all were mice and rats. If you find yourself feeling less sympathetic, you are not alone. Public sentiment over these incidents varies widely by species. One official conveyed this distinction well when he addressed reporters about the incident at Wyeth. After explaining that the number of deaths due to mechanical failure in a lab was "not unusual," he went on to say, "Horrible things have happened with nonhuman primates dying, and this is perceived to be different." In other words, mice are expendable. Why should anyone care?

The lack of systematic reporting of the total number of animals used in laboratories in the United States makes it difficult to put these deaths into perspective. Estimates vary widely, putting the numbers between seventeen and eighty million a year.[4] The vast majority of these animals—about 85 percent—are rats and mice. The remaining 15 percent include other small rodents, dogs, cats, rabbits, monkeys, and chimpanzees. Mice and rats are considered the "heroes" of modern biomedical research, routinely "sacrificed," to use the industry's term, by the millions.[5] In this light, why should the deaths of a few thousand mice in a disaster even raise an eyebrow?

In this chapter, I argue that their deaths should do more: they should raise objections and outrage. Animal research is funded with large sums of private and public money. When animals die in experiments, it is with the understanding that there was some payoff, in human terms, for the loss. I say this is the "understanding" because I recognize that many would argue that animal research has not benefited humans. I do not intend to settle that matter here, but I want to point out that, regardless of the actual payoffs of animal research, the assumption is that it does bring benefit. However, when animals destined for research die in disasters, there is no payoff and no accountability for the loss. The animals are replaced, at great expense, even if the facility in which the replacement animals are used makes them vulnerable to the same hazards. This process is especially likely to occur when the animals involved are rats and mice, who are not even defined as "animals" under the federal Animal Welfare Act. Thus, there are significant scientific, ethical, and moral problems with animal research, and along with these are also political problems. No case provides a better example than that of the laboratory rats who were victims of Tropical Storm Allison.

For two weeks in early June 2001, Tropical Storm Allison drenched the Gulf Coast region. As it moved across Texas, it stalled over Houston for several days, dropping record amounts of rain on the flood-prone area. On Friday, June 8, the storm moved north, giving residents the impression that the worst had passed. Later that same day, however, Allison drifted south again, dumping torrential rain on the area throughout the early morning hours of Saturday, June

9. The rainfall overwhelmed the city's flood-control systems. The most severe damage occurred in two areas: downtown Houston and the Texas Medical Center (TMC), often described as the "city within a city." The TMC is the world's largest medical complex. Its nearly seven-hundred-acre campus encompasses thirteen hospitals, two medical schools, four schools of nursing, and numerous research facilities, including Baylor College of Medicine and the University of Texas Health Sciences Center at Houston. Consequently, the TMC houses countless animals used in research.

The TMC sits in a bowl-shaped depression. Through it runs Brays Bayou (sometimes spelled "Braes"), part of the network of bayous, gulleys, and culverts that makes up Houston's drainage system. The region regularly receives intense rainfall; in Harris County, where Houston is located, floods occur five to eight times a year and reports of destructive flooding date to 1843, shortly after the city's founding. To complicate flood management efforts, Houston has experienced tremendous population growth, nearly doubling its population during the 1950s and again in the 1960s. As the population has grown and the urban areas have expanded, the amount of cement and blacktop infrastructure has only increased the risk of flooding. When Brays Bayou was built in 1968, it could contain water from a one-hundred-year flood event. However, rapid development has "degenerated" its capacity. Engineering studies indicated that, by 1999, Brays Bayou could barely handle the water from a ten-year flood.[6] As Allison stalled over Houston in June 2001, the city received 80 percent of its total annual rainfall in five days. Most of the bayous overtopped their banks, and several exceeded one-hundred-year flood levels. In downtown Houston, surface water run-off alone reached depths of five feet.

When the storm moved north and the rain abated on Friday, June 8, TMC employees headed home for the weekend. Thus, few were on campus when the flooding began. According to reports, many tried to reach the complex but found the area roads inundated and impassable. Houston has the world's largest pedestrian tunnel system. At the TMC, the tunnels provided a conduit that carried filthy water directly into the buildings. Water poured down the ramps leading to loading docks below ground level. It flowed into subterranean parking garages. It knocked down concrete walls and pushed open doors to the buildings. Many of the facilities lost power, and backup generators failed because hurricane planning recommended placing them in basements, where they were quickly submerged.

Twenty-two people died in the flooding in Houston and nearly seven thousand required rescue.[7] Several hospitals within the TMC relocated patients. Although no human lives were lost at the TMC, over 35,000 animals died there. The basement of the Baylor College of Medicine's research facilities housed 120,000 animals. Because of the flooding, the staff member scheduled to care for the large animals, including cows, dogs, and pigs, over the weekend, could not reach the TMC. Fortunately, the facility manager, Dan Martin, had checked into a nearby hotel. His pager awoke him in the early morning hours, and when he arrived at the building, he began to rescue animals. He saved 13 dogs and, when he met up with three faculty members, the team saved a cow, around 25 rabbits, and 4 pigs. By this time, water was rising too fast to continue. The majority of the animals at Baylor were mice, as is true of most medical research facilities and in research overall. The water levels eventually reached eighteen to twenty-four feet. As Martin reported, he found it "impossible to tackle anything concerning the mice." None survived the ordeal. According to reports, 30,000 mice presumably drowned. Those who did not drown in floodwaters count as what Baylor officials consider "residual losses," dying from disease, starvation, or dehydration. Numerous birds starved to death because of the power outage. Some reports put the number of animals who died at Baylor as high as 90,000.[8]

Nearby, at the Center for Laboratory Animal Medicine and Care of the University of Texas Health Science Center, the scene was repeated. Here, too, the major animal care facility was located in the basement. At midnight on Friday, June 8, the facility manager had reported that all was well. By two A.M. on Saturday, the basement had begun to flood. Personnel who lived nearby tried to reach the facility but were kept away by waist-deep water. By 3:30

A.M., twenty-two feet of water submerged the basement and ground level. When the recovery operations began on Monday, June 11, over ten million gallons of water had to be pumped out of the basement of the facility. Seventy-eight primates, thirty-five dogs, three hundred rabbits, and thousands of mice died, bringing the total number of animal deaths to approximately five thousand. The facility was considered a total loss. The early warning system could not predict a five-hundred-year flood event and, according to Bradford Goodwin, executive director of the animal care center, the "disaster plan was extensive but worthless," because the flood prevented staff from reaching the facility. He explained:

> Our disaster plan had extremely detailed plans as to where each animal was to be moved in the event of a hurricane or flood, etc. Each animal room was matched with another room on an upper floor of the Medical School. This plan was based on advance knowledge of an impending storm using the assumption that a few hours would be available to move the animals. In this case, there was no adequate warning and when the flood waters filled the facilities, personnel were confined to their homes.[9]

A similar "we never expected this" attitude appeared during Hurricane Katrina. Whereas Houston is flood-prone, New Orleans sits below sea level. The "big one" was just a matter of time. Yet, when the LSU's Health Sciences Center in downtown New Orleans flooded, it took everyone by surprise. One LSU official said that the water "came up so quickly that the human beings who were the caretakers for [the] animals were ordered to leave immediately."[10] None of the eight thousand mice, rats, dogs and monkeys who remained in the labs survived.

When reports of the loss of animal lives in laboratories appeared in the media after Tropical Storm Allison, they typically did so in the context of lost "research." For example, the *Houston Chronicle* reported, "Lab Animals Drown; Medical Research Lost."[11] Few recognize the loss of animal lives, and most make the animals invisible.

For example, the *Washington Times* reported, "Floods Ruin Years of Health Research; Texas Medical Center Was Inundated."[12] In the sole extant article that acknowledges the deaths of individual animals, a University of Texas veterinarian admits, "'We Failed Them, and It's Terrible'; Drownings of 78 Monkeys, 35 Dogs Lamented by UT Veterinary Official."[13] He apparently did not lament the mice. Presumably, the dogs and primates were thus mourned in a memorial service held in October 2001 at the University of Texas facility. Over 150 people reportedly attended. According to Goodwin, the event was an effort to "bring this tragedy to closure."[14] In other words, it was time to get back to business as usual. According to a 2004 report from the University of Texas Health Sciences Center, "Animal research is going strong." Goodwin said, "We actually have more animals today than we did at the time of disaster."[15]

Species Matters

The "get back to business" approach evident in Goodwin's remark highlights the meaning that the animals in the laboratory have for researchers. These animals have a place along the sociozoologic scale. By helping to maintain the institution of biomedical research, they become less like animals and more like tools. Their responses are transformed into "data," and their very bodies become "cell lines." The meanings we attribute to animals determine their moral status. For example, consider the numerous roles and labels we assign to rodents.[16] A mouse or rat can be a pet, in which case he or she has a name and is considered an individual. When a pet mouse or rat dies, a burial may occur, perhaps in the family garden and complete with mourners. In such instances, at least some members of the family experience the event as a loss. In other instances, however, mice and rats are seen as pests. They eat food meant for humans. Through their travels, they spread diseases that threaten humans. These animals have no individual names. They are considered disgusting and loathsome. When they die, their death sometimes comes by poisoning. Other times, they die in ineffective but commonplace snap traps that break bones but seldom deliver enough force placed strategically to result in instant death. Alternatively, they die in sticky traps, which are "essentially a rodent form of flypaper."[17] They become stuck on strong adhesive and their struggles to escape only cause more of their body surface to adhere. Anyone finding a mouse or rat on a sticky trap can see evidence of suffering. Treating a dog, cat, or other animal to a death by poison or entrapment would constitute cruelty, by the laws of any state. No one mourns the deaths of mice and rats considered pests, rather than pets.

Neither does anyone mourn the deaths of mice raised to feed carnivorous species, such as snakes (and some lizards and toads). Most snakes must eat live prey. For snakes in captivity, "feeder" mice can be adults, juveniles, or newborns, called "pinkies" because they are still hairless. The competition between prey and predator in captivity, both of whom can hold the same status as pets, raises unique moral issues. To feed the snake, the mouse must die. If the mouse lives, the snake will starve. The mouse's fate depends on whether we considered him or her food or pet. The people who feed the snake might feel disgust or fascination about the act of feeding live prey, but no one who grieves for the mouse can care for snakes for very long. Finally, tremendous numbers of mice exist as research tools. They are not considered research subjects, for doing so would grant them far more agency than they have. These mice are not pets; they do not count as individuals. Indeed, individuality is exactly what scientists strive to avoid in what are known as "animal models." The mouse's journey to the animal-model-of-choice illustrates how scientists regard them, how the strength of the scientific discourse influences popular thought, and why they die in such large numbers, whether in disasters or ordinary laboratory experience.

Producing Mice, Producing Science

The species of mouse most commonly used in laboratories is the white mouse, or the albino strain of *Mus musculus*. Originally from Asia, mice spread across Europe and came to the New World as stowaways in the 1500s. During a breeding craze in the nineteenth century that also gave us most of today's breeds of dogs and cats, amateur rodent enthusiasts bred "fancy" strains from wild mice and rats, usually selecting for coat color. Early in the twentieth century, a Harvard graduate student named Clarence Cook Little obtained a pair of mice with well-documented bloodlines and began breeding them for his research on genetics.[18] Mice reproduce quickly, reaching sexual maturity around six weeks of age. They have litters of at least four and as many as ten pups, and they can easily produce a dozen litters a year. Their reproductive capacity made them the species of choice for students of mammalian genetics. Little bred brother to sister for over twenty generations and selected the most vigorous offspring. By using the inbreeding techniques already employed by fanciers, he engineered strains that frequently developed cancerous mammary tumors. At the same time, Little and others strove to define cancer in genetic terms.[19] As Karen Rader explains, "The problem thus defined, inbred mice were the required standard" for cancer research.[20] The mice developed tumors, bred quickly enough for researchers to observe the disease's generational course, and, through inbreeding, had the stable genetic material that eliminated unwanted variability. Most important, because mice are mammals, scientists presumed that diseases in mice follow courses similar to those that afflict human beings. Mice became a morally acceptable stand-in for humans in medical research. Consequently, researchers created numerous distinct strains of mice for particular research applications. These include nude (or hairless) mice, which lack a thymus and thus do not reject implanted tumors from other species, such as humans. Severe combined immune deficient mice are a "souped-up" version of the nude mouse, valued for studies of immunodeficiency.

The growth of research in molecular biology during the 1970s and 1980s created even greater demand for and supply of mice because of the relative ease with which their genes can be modified at the molecular level.[21] The "knockout" mouse has a particular gene inactivated, demonstrating the behavior, appearance, or biology of an individual who lacks that gene. Genes from other rodents or other species, including humans and even jellyfish, can be inserted into mice to merge with other genes.[22] Because large numbers of rodents kept in close quarters present ideal conditions for disease outbreaks, breeders developed "specific pathogen free" mice, which have none of the bacterial or viral pathogens carried by "conventional" mice. "Gnotobiotic" mice are delivered by C-section; the mother dies in the process. The sterile uterus is placed in a sterile environment. Scientists can infect the fetuses with just a single microbe, allowing for the study of the effects of only the one organism. Scientists engineered "transgenic" mice by altering embryos with one or more genes that produce a trait of interest, such as a predisposition to develop human breast cancer. Selective breeding results in generations of mice characterized by the genetic alteration. "Chimeric" mice are produced by altering the DNA sequences of embryonic mouse stem cells and adding them to mouse embryos. Some of the offspring of chimeric mice will have the altered DNA sequences.

The production of rodents, particularly mice, for laboratories has become a huge industry. Researchers can consult extensive catalogues and choose from over thirty-five hundred strains.[23] Mice became the species of choice for most laboratory research because of the convergence of three trends concerning how scientific work takes place. Two of these were apparent in Little's efforts to develop inbred mice. The first is the need for standardized equipment, materials, and procedures. Although taken for granted today, scientists did not seek standardization until the mid-to-late-nineteenth century. Previously, researchers had used a variety of species in their experiments.[24] As other aspects of the lab, such as machinery for measurement, became standardized, the next logical step was to standardize the animals used in research. Scientists moved away from using a variety of species, and the purpose-bred mouse or rat became the basic "laboratory animal." The commercial production of rodents, who reproduce quickly and respond well to selective breeding, met the new demand for standardization. In the transition from diversity to generality, rodents used in research lost their identity as individual animals and became "tools of the trade, part of the apparatus of science," even referred to as "test tubes with tails."[25] The rodents used in research become something other than animals, for they "have no counterparts in nature."[26]

A second, closely related trend involves assumptions about the generalizability of animal models to human diseases and conditions. Scientists use millions of animals, particularly mice, because they believe they can extrapolate the results to human beings. Although some researchers conduct studies on animals to understand clinical conditions that affect animals, most scientists do not study mice to learn about rodents but to generalize their findings to human problems. The vast majority of research involves the assumption that the knowledge gained can benefit humans. Because of the moral problems inherent in using human subjects for invasive, harmful research, scientists cannot experiment directly on people. Moreover, most researchers consider studies conducted on humans "scientifically second-rate."[27] The inability to control for different lifestyles, environments, and histories introduces numerous confounding factors into any clinical study using human subjects. Researchers assume that the causal mechanisms at work in disease and the treatment response are analogous in animals and humans.[28] In addition, because researchers can stabilize genetic background and living conditions among animal subjects, studies using animal subjects are, at least in theory, more likely to produce reliable data. Finally, because the subjects are not humans, their use raises no strong moral objections. In biomedical and ethical terms, then, the mouse "stands in" for a human being. To be sure, few if any researchers believe that mice and humans are identical organisms. However, they do not see the differences between species "as undermining the legitimacy of animal experimentation," and they believe that they accommodate differences by adjusting for scale.[29] Belief in the generalizability of animal models to human conditions is part of the "institutional thinking" surrounding scientific knowledge. The training of researchers incorporates the use of animal models early. Along with understanding how to use machines and instruments and how to write a scientific paper, knowing how to use animal models constitutes the skill set necessary for "doing" science.[30] Many scientists acquire a significant stake in continuing to use animals in their research not only because of their commitment to the paradigm that endorses their use but also because journals and funding agencies commonly expect or even require animal models. Researchers seeking to publish or receive tenure, promotion, or grants are unlikely to try alternatives. Thus, the suitability of animal models for studying human conditions goes virtually unquestioned. The American Medical Association and the international research society Sigma Xi staunchly defend the use of animals in research.[31] The biomedical community overall asserts that most modern medical advances have resulted from animal experimentation. From this perspective, the benefits to humans outweigh any harm to animals. Questioning these prevailing assumptions about the use of animals would threaten the current paradigm of biomedical research altogether.[32] Criticism of the generalizability of animal models typically comes from those outside the scientific community, whose views the "insiders" thus deem unscientific or even antiscience.

Finally, it does not seem coincidental that as the use of mice increased, animal welfare legislation determined that the status of "animal," and therefore the protection extended to them, does not apply to mice and rats bred for research. In the United States, the initial legislation we know as the Animal Welfare Act aimed at preventing the theft of pets for use in experiments. This issue came to public attention in the mid-1960s through two popular magazines. An exposé in *Sports Illustrated* reported that a missing Dalmatian named Pepper had appeared in a local newspaper's photograph of a dog dealer's truck.[33] When Pepper's family went to retrieve her, the dog dealer turned them away from his "farm." U.S. Representative Joseph Resnick (D-New York) also attempted to retrieve Pepper and was denied entrance. Along the way, Pepper died in an experimental procedure at Montefiore Hospital in New York. Soon after, Resnick introduced a bill to require U.S. Department of Agriculture licensing and inspection of dog and cat dealers and the laboratories that purchased them. Four months later, *Life* magazine called attention to how research facilities procured their animals, particularly dogs and cats.[34] The article, entitled "Concentration Camps for Lost and Stolen Pets," exposed the abuse and neglect at the "farm" of a Maryland dealer who obtained "subjects" for research programs. In response largely to the articles, Congress passed the Laboratory Animal Welfare Act (Public Law 89-554) in 1966, authorizing the U.S. Department of Agriculture to regulate the "handling, care, treatment, and transportation of animals by dealers and research facilities." The act applies to dogs, cats, and "certain animals intended for use in research facilities." It defines "animal" as "live dogs, cats, monkeys (nonhuman primate mammals), guinea pigs, hamsters, and rabbits."[35] Amendments added in 1970 shorten the law's name to the Animal Welfare Act and define an "animal" as "any live or dead dog, cat, monkey (nonhuman primate mammal), guinea pig, hamster, rabbit, or such other warm-blooded animal."[36] A 2002 amendment removed any vagueness about which species constitutes "animals" by "specifically excluding birds, rats of the genus *Rattus*, and mice of the genus *Mus*, bred for use in research."[37] In other words, the Animal Welfare Act covers only six species used in research—dogs, cats, nonhuman primates, rabbits, hamsters, and guinea pigs—but not those used most often and in the greatest numbers. Notably—and conveniently—it excludes the very animals researchers have created. By excluding "purpose-bred" mice and rats, the act makes moral status rest on the animals' reason for being in the lab, as if it were a matter of their choosing.[38]

The exclusion of purpose-bred animals and their rapidly increasing use in research points to a paradox in animal welfare policy. There has always been some public opposition to the most inhumane uses of animals in experiments, and this opposition prompted researchers to seek ways to quell some of the criticism. The solution is known as the Three R's: researchers should *reduce* the number of animals used in experiments, *refine* procedures to minimize animal pain and suffering, and *replace* animal subjects with nonanimal alternatives where scientifically feasible.[39] The Three R's represent an attempt to minimize animal suffering in ways that still permit research. During the sweeping 1985 amendments of the Animal Welfare Act, Congress incorporated the Three

R's into the law in various provisions.[40] What is most significant, the 1985 amendments mandated the formation of institutional animal care and use committees, or IACUCs, which review protocols for animal research. However, the Animal Welfare Act does not apply to mice, rats, or birds, who constitute the majority of animals used in research. Moreover, with the rapid growth of the biotechnology industry, mice and rats are being produced in dramatically increasing numbers. While legislation aims to decrease the use of animals, the trend has been to use them in greater numbers by not giving the majority of them legal standing. When these animals die in disasters rather than experiments, the only regrets are over "lost research."

Most university-based facilities must also follow guidelines established by the National Institutes of Health (NIH) and its parent institution, the Public Health Service.[41] Whereas the Animal Welfare Act was imposed on labs by Congress, the NIH guidelines were created from within the scientific community as a form of self-regulation.[42] Although I will not compare the two sets of regulations in detail here, I do want to make three related points. The NIH guidelines, in contrast to the Animal Welfare Act, include rats, mice, and birds. The NIH is the largest provider of funds to medical research facilities in the United States, and the grant money they dole out comes from tax dollars.[43] Finally, because the guidelines apply to institutions receiving federal funds, which include university campuses, the NIH can—at least in theory—withhold funding from institutions that fail to comply.[44] Consequently, animal advocates have appealed to the NIH for sanctions following the deaths of animals in disasters. Their efforts highlight the different ways the two groups view animals and animal experimentation.

Seeking Accountability

On learning of the memorial service for the animals lost in Tropical Storm Allison, Theodora Capaldo, executive director of the New England Anti-Vivisection Society, wrote to the editor of the *Houston Chronicle*, stating that the "public show of sentiment is suspect and is, in fact, a manipulation of public opinion about how researchers care for animals." She continues:

> If their attachment were real, why wasn't an emergency evacuation plan in place? Why were the animals abandoned to certain death? Researchers at University of Texas and Baylor College "lost the animals entrusted to [their] care." Why isn't this neglect being viewed as criminal animal cruelty? Why are those responsible not being called to task? The answer is simple: because they were "laboratory animals"—therefore, no one has done anything wrong![45]

The International Primate Protection League urged its members and the public to write letters calling for an investigation of the deaths and the firing of any employees found responsible for the lack of preparation and the failure to evacuate the animals. Bradford Goodwin, of the University of Texas, received over a hundred letters. People for the Ethical Treatment of Animals (PETA) contacted the NIH, asking them to require that federally funded projects evacuate their animals in impending disasters. The NIH claimed not to have the authority to make such stipulations.[46] Similarly, the Physicians' Committee for Responsible Medicine appealed to the presidents of the University of Texas Health Science Center and Baylor College of Medicine, urging them not to replace the animals who died in flood. The committee recommended that the institutions instead turn to human clinical trials, epidemiological studies, in vitro research, and the techniques emerging from the human genome project. The group suggested that the flood had presented an opportunity for the TMC institutions to become leaders in alternatives to the use of animals in research. Instead, the University of Texas was using more animals in 2004 than at the time of the storm. The response to the disaster had been simply not to house animals in the basement.

In response to the deaths of eight thousand animals at LSU's Health Sciences Center labs following Hurricane Katrina, PETA took similar but stronger steps. The group contacted Michael Johanns, secretary of agriculture, requesting that the U.S. Department of Agriculture charge LSU with violations of the Animal Welfare Act. They also wrote to Mike Leavitt, secretary of the U.S. Department of Health and Human Services, which administers the Public Health Service, of which the NIH is an agency. PETA's letter requested that "the Department of Health and Human Services refuse to provide federal funding for the building or rebuilding of research facilities in high-risk areas of the country." The letter asked that the agency withhold federal funds from LSU "because of its dereliction of duty to the animals abandoned and left to drown, suffocate, starve, and die of dehydration." PETA also wrote to Louisiana's attorney general, Charles Foti, asking him to charge LSU officials with cruelty for abandoning the animals in their labs. Under Louisiana law, cruelty includes abandoning an animal without arranging for its care. In addition, the group wrote to the chancellor of LSU calling for the firing of two officials at the Health Sciences Center.[47] None of these actions was taken. The letters also pointed out that the animals should have been evacuated or euthanized.

In calling for the withholding of federal funds, animal advocacy groups used the only tools available to them. Funding for animal research comes from tax dollars, and, as members of the public, animal advocates can object to providing additional money to rebuild what they see as a deeply flawed practice. Because these agencies are part of and invested in animal research as an institution, they cannot adequately respond to opponents' charges—even when those charges do not call for the elimination of all research on animals. In my research, I found no cases in which federal funds were withheld, nor did I find any cases in which labs were charged with violations of the Animal Welfare Act in the aftermath of a disaster. Indeed, following Hurricane Katrina, the procedures for reporting animal deaths did not apply. Usually, animal deaths in research labs that are unrelated to the experiments for which they were designated must be reported "promptly" and "without delay" to the NIH's Office of Laboratory Animal Welfare. The list of reportable situations includes "conditions that jeopardize the health or well-being of animals, including natural disasters, accidents, and mechanical failures, resulting in actual harm or death to animals."[48] However, the office waived the requirement following Katrina because of the severity of the storm and the scattering of LSU staff across the country.

Attempts by animal advocates to hold someone accountable highlight the contrasting meanings of animals in laboratories. As earlier outlined, researchers are committed to a paradigm that incorporates the use of animals in their experiments. Their justification is essentially threefold: humans and nonhuman animals are biologically similar; because we cannot experiment on humans, we should use animals as models; the benefits to human beings are worth the suffering and deaths of any number of animals. From this view, any attempt to curtail the use of animals would impede research and compromise the quality of human life. Put on the defensive, the research community proclaims that "all science is excellent and some is especially so."[49] Researchers depict the opposition as misinformed, unscientific, sentimental, trivial, and holding unrealistic views about how research operates. They portray groups such as PETA as having misplaced priorities, valuing animals more than human beings. In contrast, animal advocates paint all researchers with the same brush and see only exaggeration, flawed science, and immorality.

The defenders of animal experimentation maintain that the practice plays a critical and indispensable role in improving the quality of human life. Its opponents, and some historians of medicine, claim that the defenders have exaggerated its benefits. For example, the American Medical Association credits animal research with extending the human life-span by helping to conquer numerous major childhood diseases, such as smallpox, diphtheria, scarlet fever, whooping cough, and measles. Medical historians note, however, that the decline in mortality from these diseases occurred before treatments and vaccinations were developed.[50] With many diseases, such as pneumonia and even cancer, preventive measures have reduced mortality more significantly than have interventions drawn from animal research.[51] Opponents also argue that research on animals has had a much less significant role than its defenders would have us believe. Most of the significant advances in medicine have come from studies of humans, not animals. For instance, Neal Barnard, president of the Physicians Committee for Responsible Medicine (PCRM), pointed out that "the risk factors that contribute to heart disease were identified in human population studies and tested in human clinical trials. Animal studies offer no greater insight into this issue."[52] Because those who conduct research on animals do not critically examine the practice, they continue to use animals largely because it would be politically, economically, and institutionally difficult to question the status quo.[53] And because there are no systematic reviews of the research conducted on animals, many experiments duplicate existing results and pose questions already answered.[54] A review of highly cited animal studies published in leading scientific journals reports that only about one-third of the research was replicated among human subjects. The authors conclude that "patients and physicians should remain cautious about extrapolating the findings of prominent animal research to the care of human disease."[55] In addition, opponents argue that animals do not respond to drugs in the same ways that humans do and therefore conclusions drawn from animal research have sometimes resulted in harm to human beings. Numerous medications that have been successful in animal tests and have thus reached the market, they point out, have resulted in human illness and death. One notable case concerns the drug thalidomide, widely marketed during the 1950s to pregnant women for morning sickness, particularly in Britain. In tests, animals tolerated massive doses of the drug; when taken by pregnant women, it resulted in serious birth defects. A recent example involves the arthritis drug Vioxx, which was taken off the market after it caused an estimated sixty thousand deaths. Animal research had shown it to be safe and beneficial—to animals' hearts.[56]

Finally, opponents criticize animal research on moral grounds. Many point out that, regardless of the promise the research holds, it is morally objectionable to use nonhuman animals for human ends. According to opponents, we cannot justify experimenting on animals simply because they are not humans. Most people would agree that killing an animal, say, a dog, simply because I might find it fun to do so is morally wrong. We recognize that the death is a loss, even if it is a less significant loss than that associated with a human death. Our objections to such behavior are enshrined in laws against cruelty. Thus, as a society, we place limits on what we can do to animals. Scholars from disparate backgrounds have argued that animals have at least some moral standing, and some take this to the point of granting animals rights.[57] There is no single quality that all humans possess, which consequently gives all humans greater moral weight than any other animal. To experiment on animals simply because they are not humans is considered speciesist, and species, like the traits of race and sex, is morally irrelevant.[58]

Proponents of animal research portray the work they do as noble, and the suffering and deaths of animals as heroic "sacrifices" on behalf of humankind. They see the opposition as misinformed and sentimental, and a threat to the scientific enterprise. Worse, they lump groups that use violence and intimidation together with those who oppose the research but would never break into a lab, and those who support most kinds of research but want stricter welfare standards and greater scrutiny. Opponents of animal research see the enterprise as cruel and misguided and the researchers as "sadistic fools."[59] The positions appear to leave very little room for a middle ground. However, as Julian Groves found in his study of those on both sides of the debate, in reality, the lines are not so clearly drawn.[60] Animal researchers frequently express care about and concern for animals. Activists often use scientific language to justify their opposition to experimentation. Like Groves, I would argue that there is a point of consensus: both sides care about the well-being of animals.[61]

Reducing Animals' Vulnerability in Labs

We make animals vulnerable in many ways by confining them in research labs. And we make them vulnerable to whatever experimental procedures researchers may enact on them. We do this so that humans do not face the same risks. However, by confining animals in labs, we also make them vulnerable in ways unrelated to the reason they are in the lab. Specifically, we make them vulnerable to the same hazards that humans would face in that particular setting. If the power goes out and the ventilation system fails, they suffer and even die. If the building floods, they risk death by drowning. In the research for this chapter, I found no instances in which people died when disasters struck research facilities, yet I uncovered cases of thousands of animal deaths. The people have one obvious advantage: they can leave the building. In contrast, the animals cannot escape and, in many cases, they could not survive outside the laboratory. Putting animals in this situation raises numerous moral questions and, clearly, many practical ones. Thus, the true solution to the various dilemmas of animal welfare during disasters in research facilities is simply not to have animals there in the first place.

This solution is unrealistic—but only for now. I would like to see animal experimentation end, and although I will not likely live long enough to see that happen, I believe it will end. The wheels are in motion to do so. As the laboratory animal veterinarian Larry Carbone explains:

> It may end, as American slavery did, because of shifting political and ethical vicissitudes. It may end, as hand-setting type did, as the technology becomes obsolete. Most likely the two will reinforce each other. Morality and politics will continue to spur the search for replacement technologies. Technological advances will strengthen the moral arguments against animal use. These dual processes are already in progress.[62]

Meanwhile, however, the trend is to use increasing numbers of small rodents, particularly genetically modified mice. The institutional thinking that requires animal models and the infrastructure built around purpose-bred animals will not change easily or quickly. New technologies, such as stem cell research, that may ultimately become alternatives to animal research will first be conducted on thousands or even millions of animals.[63] Heightened concern for bioterrorism since September 11, 2001, means that countless animals, especially nonhuman primates, will continue to be used in experiments involving anthrax, and other pathogens. As Carbone puts it, "animals *are* in laboratories, and they are going to be there for many years to come."[64] In the context of this book, the question thus becomes one of how to reduce their vulnerability when disasters strike.

I would like to propose three related steps. The first involves extending federal protection to all animals, including those bred for research. For the most part, rats, mice, and birds do not have the political capital to arouse public outrage over their treatment. If the definition of *animal* in the Animal Welfare Act were extended to include these animals, they would have at least some protection because of their position on the phylogenetic and not the sociozoologic scale. Although there has been significant resistance to this move from the scientific community as an institution, surveys indicate that most individual animal researchers support regulating rats, mice, and birds under the Animal Welfare Act.[65] Indeed, they support the change even though it would have significant potential impact on their research. In short, the opponents of animal research and its defenders agree that if research is to be conducted on animals, all species used should have at least the minimal legal protections provided by the Animal Welfare Act. In terms of disaster planning and response, this wider scope of protection would entail planning for the welfare of all animals in research facilities. Officials will claim that they already do this planning, but events such as Tropical Storm Allison and Hurricane Katrina reveal a "we never imagined" mentality that shortchanges animals in disaster planning. Including rats, mice, and birds in the Animal Welfare Act would provide a means to sanction facilities that fail to provide for the welfare of the animals under their care. For covered species, violations of the act could impose criminal and civil penalties on the research and the institution.

The loss of animals in federally funded research facilities represents a tremendous expense to the American public. More accurately, the expense comes from the replacement of animals. Thus far, there has been no way to hold facilities accountable. Tax dollars, funneled through the NIH, support research even in facilities built in high-risk areas, such as flood zones. The NIH claims it has no authority over where a facility is built or how the research is conducted. Animals are replaced without questioning whether they are needed in the studies because federal policies decide they are not "really" animals. Because the NIH has been unwilling to hold facilities accountable for disaster-related losses, including all species in the Animal Welfare Act's definition becomes especially important.

Changing the definition of *animal* in the Animal Welfare Act would provide greater protection regardless of whether a disaster strikes. However, in disaster events, this change still leaves labs holding thousands of animals in impossible situations. The second step requires taking the Three R's seriously, especially the mandate to reduce the numbers of animals used. Currently, researchers can employ several loopholes to avoid compliance.[66] Expanding the coverage of the Animal Welfare Act would eliminate one loophole. At present, because the Animal Welfare Act does not define the majority of the species used as "animals," researchers have no obligation to apply the Three R's. Simply covering additional species will not automatically mean that researchers will take steps to refine, reduce, and replace. For example, although the Animal Welfare Act requires researchers to consider replacing animal subjects with nonanimal alternatives, confirmation of this step relies on an honor system. When researchers submit their proposals for review by the IACUC, they report having considered nonanimal alternatives. The committee usually accepts that assertion, because to do otherwise would be to question (or appear to question) the design of the experiment.[67] Studies have found that researchers seldom conduct systematic reviews of previous animal experiments and instead frequently "answer questions that have already been answered."[68] Requiring that proposals for new animal experiments document that existing animal studies had been fully evaluated for validity and clinical generalizability would reduce the numbers of animals used.

These two steps aim to reduce the numbers of animals in labs and ensure that, even in the event of a disaster, all animals affected will have at least the minimal federal protection. But a third step is needed: research facilities must take the lessons of recent disasters seriously and address worst-case scenarios in their planning. It is not enough to move the animals to upper floors if the emergency generators are in the basement. It is not enough to have a plan to evacuate animals in case of flood, if the facility sits in a flood zone that may become inaccessible to the people responsible for staging the evacuation. What is enough will vary by facility, location, and potential hazards. In the ideal, we would not build research facilities on flood plains or earthquake fault lines. In reality, we must find ways of anticipating and addressing the consequences that doing so has for the animals we make vulnerable. In the concluding chapter, I discuss some of the barriers to thinking about worst-case scenarios and suggest some ways around them.

Conclusion: Noah's Task

This book opens with two questions: Do animals have a place on the ark? and if so, which animals may come aboard? I argue that animals deserve a place on the ark, for reasons that range from economic to ethical to emotional, environmental, and beyond. At the same time, I argue that our decisions about filling the ark would be easier if we did not, through our actions, make animals so vulnerable to disasters. In the preceding chapters I examine this issue of vulnerability through the two related themes. One theme concerns how the roles we assign to animals position them along the sociozoologic scale. This position determines animals' moral status, which, in turn, influences the vulnerability they face and the resources that we will marshal to rescue them. The sociozoologic location is malleable. For example, a pet dog, mouse, or rat would have a place on the ark—under most circumstances. As Hurricane Katrina showed us, we can keep even these family members off the ark when the cost of rescuing them appears too great. The picture would change if the dog, mouse, or rat were defined as a "research animal." The sociozoologic scale determines that a dog in a research facility stands a far greater chance of rescue than a mouse does. The mouse would merit rescue only after a determination was made about the value of the "data" or "cell lines" he or she embodied.

The second theme through which I examine animals' vulnerability follows from animals' moral status. It involves how we make decisions about animals' fates, which I characterize as how institutions "think" when faced with disasters. This "thinking" is shaped by economic interests, and by philosophical and political positions. For example, the poultry company sees the tornado-wrecked grower sheds as a "disposal problem" and a public relations liability. The research facility sees drowned or starving animals as lost "data." Animal advocacy groups think in terms of "rescuing" sentient beings. However, even what constitutes "rescue" depends on institutional "thinking." For example, after Hurricane Katrina, government actions (or inactions) required subsequent animal rescuers to engage in tactics such as breaking and entering, which the government denounces as "terrorism" when used by groups such as the Animal Liberation Front.[1] In the post-Katrina "rescue" efforts, animal "rescuers" broke into evacuated homes, smashed doors and windows, and used the same tactics that the Animal Liberation Front uses to "rescue" animals from research facilities. In both cases, the rescuers offered the same justifications, claiming that the animals were suffering and saving them trumped any rights to property. The difference is that in the Katrina response, the state had in effect granted permission for rescuers to engage in breaking and entering. When research labs are involved, to protect corporate interests, the government portrays the Animal Liberation Front and similar activists as "terrorists" rather than "rescuers." Always the solution involves returning to the status quo, without reducing vulnerability. The poultry company cuts its losses and brings in new flocks. The researchers order more mice. Rescuers try to raise more money and recruit more volunteers, for there will surely be a "next time." Governments push for additional regulation, as well as attendant agencies and administrators. As Charles Perrow points out, there are interests to be served, even in responding to large emergencies.[2]

Our dominion over other species ensures that human interests will always trump animal interests.

In saying this, I am not suggesting that animal interests and human interests should necessarily be equal in all disaster responses, or even in all situations. I do not propose that we allow people to die while we rescue all the animals. However, some animal rescue will always be necessary, and in what follows, I offer ideas—some concrete, others less so—about how to improve our efforts.

What We Know and How We Can Use It

Companion Animals

Our relationships with companion animals give us numerous reasons to save them. Because we have enlisted dogs, cats, and other species to be our companions, we have an ethical imperative to rescue them if the need arises. We also have psychosocial reasons to save them; disasters involve stress and trauma, and the loss of a beloved companion animal can only add to the emotional burden. Moreover, as the unprecedented post-Katrina rescue effort showed, it takes significant time, effort, labor, and money to save animals left behind. As the events in Dayton, Ohio, and Weyauwega, Wisconsin, showed, people will risk their lives and imperil the lives of others to save their animals. With the passing of the Pets Evacuation and Transportation Standards (PETS) Act, the federal government has implemented policy to prevent another Katrina for animals. However, the law only ensures that people will be allowed to evacuate with their animals. Companion animal guardians must take steps to be ready to evacuate. My recommendation is deceptively simple: people who have companion animals need to assess the type of risks they face and prepare for emergencies. For any risk, the preparation involves the following:

- Have sufficient food, water, litter, and litter pans on hand to care for animals for three days if required to "shelter in place" or remain at home until the danger has passed. Nonperishables can be acquired beforehand, and in most instances, depending on the amount of notice provided, any perishables can be procured at the last minute.

- Have identification for all animals. Ideally, this would be a permanent identifier, such as a microchip or tattoo, in addition to a collar with visible ID tags. The microchip or tattoo should be recorded with a national registry, which also lists out-of-area contacts, such as friends or family members, in case telephone service is disrupted. It is useful also to have recent photographs of all animals for identification purposes. If a cat escapes from a carrier and runs away, the picture can help identify him or her.
- Have a supply of any medications, along with copies of veterinary records.
- Have leashes for dogs and carriers for cats. Households with multiple cats should have ample carriers. Many people have only one carrier despite having multiple cats because they use the carriers for trips to the vet, one at a time. Each cat should have his or her own carrier.
- Have a plan of where to go if you must evacuate and how you will get there. Although many situations will involve "sheltering in place," other events could require evacuation. Identify friends and family who would house you and your animals in such a situation. Keep a list of pet-friendly hotels.
- Have a plan for what to do if a disaster strikes while you are not home. Know where animals will be sheltered after evacuation.

In practice, these are easy steps, requiring only a few hours of work. Nevertheless, I call this recommendation "deceptively simple" because the challenge involves how to prompt people to prepare— before the crisis, when there will be many competing priorities. The question of how to get people to prepare for something that may never happen has puzzled disaster researchers for decades.

Inertia makes it too easy to do nothing. Although people cannot be required to prepare for a disaster, I offer a few suggestions for how to encourage them to do so.

I suggest that we integrate veterinarians into the disaster planning process by making them the link between state and local emergency managers and animal guardians. Many veterinarians are already involved in local, regional, and national disaster response efforts through organizations such as the American Veterinary Medical Association, and their assistance is invaluable. This recommendation simply moves their involvement back a step. In short, all vets can be a conduit for information about regional hazards and the importance of preparation. At the time of an animal's annual veterinary examination, the vet could explain the potential hazards within an area, such as hurricane, flood, tornado, or ice storm, and the recommended steps for preparation. A brochure, possibly produced by state or county animal response teams, could provide a checklist for planning. The brochure would include the list of items recommended for preparation, as well as the locations of pet-friendly hotels and other resources in the area. Although all this information is available on many Web sites, integrating it into the annual vet exam brings it to the guardian, instead of requiring him or her to take the initiative and look for it. Schools of veterinary medicine and professional associations could assist with making this a normative part of a routine vet exam.

A host of other incentives could encourage guardians of animals to prepare. For example, across the United States, people have learned to change the batteries in smoke alarms twice a year, when they change their clocks in spring and fall. Although this campaign has not resulted in perfect compliance, it has raised awareness and routinized a simple but easy to forget safety procedure. Similarly, emergency planning offices (even FEMA, the Federal Emergency Management Agency) could piggyback onto this semi-annual event to inform people about planning for disasters. They could provide information about preparation for disasters twice a year in newspapers and on community Web sites. The information would be tailored to the hazards faced in the region. The timing is ideal because many natural hazards differ by season. Pet supply stores could offer lists of what items to stock up on. Along another line, insurance companies could offer a modest discount to homeowners who have disaster plans in place for their animals. Verifying the plans could involve a checklist of requirements such as documentation of animals' microchip or tattoo information, the telephone numbers of out-of-area emergency contacts, and possession of sufficient carriers and leashes.

The PETS Act aims to ensure that a Katrina-like situation will not occur again. The responses to hurricanes Gustav and Ike showed dramatic improvement. But even with legislation, the burden of responsibility remains where it should be: with the guardians (or owners) of the animals. It will take a combination of information, education, and incentives to prompt people to accept that responsibility.

Animals Raised for Food

Throughout the book, I emphasize reducing animals' vulnerability to disasters by reducing the numbers of animals we use in various contexts. Intensive agriculture, or the system known as "factory farming," is an obvious place to start. When disasters strike agricultural facilities of any kind, three problems arise: the possibility that animals will have to be evacuated, waste pollution, and carcass disposal. Because of the tremendous number of animals housed in factory farms, or CAFOs (concentrated animal feeding operations), these issues can quickly get out of control. Besides having a horrific impact on animals, disasters affect regional public health by polluting air and water. Eliminating factory farming altogether would be ideal. As I discuss in Chapter 2, sustainable farming practices would make animals and people less vulnerable, in normal times as well as in disasters. And although a move to sustainability will not address the numerous thorny animal rights issues related to our use of animals, it will improve the welfare of animals in disasters. It does not entail radical or extremist views; it is an idea whose time has come.

I argue that sustainable agriculture needs consumers willing to purchase its products. I suggest that a labeling system be implemented for all animal products that enables consumers to make purchases that are consistent with their moral commitments. In addition to consumer support, sustainability requires that certain agricultural policy issues be addressed. Some of these involve reforming the system that provides direct and indirect subsidies to industrial livestock operations. Currently, these subsidies allow corporations that run CAFOs to buy feed crops for 20 to 25 percent under cost of production. Underpriced feed, subsidized by taxpayers, has meant artificially low costs for CAFO operators and artificially low prices for meat raised in industrial conditions.[3] Subsidies have pushed more small farmers out of diversified production, in which they raise both crops and livestock, and into the production of commodity crops exclusively. Removing the subsidies could make diversified small farms profitable again.[4] At the very least, it would make factory farming less profitable. Moreover, as Michael Pollan writes, it would require developing "a new set of incentives that would encourage farmers to grow real food and take good care of their land."[5]

More directly related to disaster management, the federal government should establish stringent standards for the "carrying capacity," or permissible numbers of animals and amount of waste relative to features such as geology and groundwater. The standards should not permit operations to house large numbers of animals in floodplains or otherwise fragile locations. Currently, the federal government does not regulate CAFOs unless they have a record of polluting, and even then, enforcement can take years. Consistent federal standards are necessary to avoid loopholes at the state or regional level. As the Pew Commission reports, many facilities are situated in poor communities through a combination of the promise of job creation and the offer of tax incentives.[6] Thus, legislators may hesitate to refuse to allow a potential primary employer to operate in their jurisdiction. The agriculture lobby has also worked to bypass local control over zoning. However, because taxpayers bear the external costs of CAFOs, state and local legislators actually have a strong incentive to favor small-sized operations. For example, large CAFOs produce overwhelming amounts of waste, which is stored in lagoons or spread on the land (or both). The volume of waste contains far more nutrients than the land can absorb, resulting in contamination of soil and surface and groundwater. The Union of Concerned Scientists reports that remediation of the leaching of waste from dairy and hog CAFOs in Kansas alone will cost that state's taxpayers $56 million. Based on these figures, which are conservative because Kansas is not a major dairy- or hog-producing state, the estimated nationwide clean-up costs in these two industries would exceed $4.1 billion. In other examples, pollutants from CAFOs have caused a steady decline in the Chesapeake Bay blue crab industry. They have also contributed to a "dead zone" in the Gulf of Mexico, resulting in losses in fishing and shrimping. In short, state and local governments considering whether to allow a CAFO in their region should not have to weigh the promise of jobs against potential social and economic losses. Strict federal standards should guide their decisions. State and local governments could establish stricter criteria, but they should be at least as stringent as the federal regulations.

Regulations for siting CAFOs could reduce the environmental toll during disasters by reducing the numbers of animals in a particular geographic location. Reforming taxpayer subsidies would encourage sustainable animal husbandry. Together these shifts would reduce animals' vulnerability. They would, for example, reduce the risk of disease, and the risks associated with the drugs routinely used to prevent them, both of which also put human populations at risk. A third policy that can support sustainability and reduce vulnerability involves reciprocity of slaughterhouse inspection. Ready access to local slaughterhouses with U.S. Department of Agriculture (USDA) certification would improve small farmers' access to markets for sustainably raised meat. Measures to provide such access were approved in the 2008 federal farm bill, but much work remains to be done before the effects are seen. For meat to be sold across state lines or in foreign countries, the USDA requires that animals be slaughtered, processed, and packaged at USDA-approved slaughter facilities. However, large companies own most of the approved facilities and these facilities have become increasingly concentrated in particular areas of the country. They process mostly their own "captive supply," or animals raised by the company's own producers. In keeping with the "get big or get out" dictum of industrial agriculture, many facilities will not accept small numbers of animals. Thus, many farmers do not have access to USDA-certified slaughterhouses. They have to truck their animals long distances to be slaughtered. Some have solved this problem by forming co-ops and pooling their animals for slaughter in USDA-approved facilities.

The existing system has posed a significant obstacle to sustainability because it makes it difficult for consumers to purchase meat from farmers who support good husbandry without making direct arrangements with that farmer. To sell meat in local retail outlets, farmers must either transport their live animals to state-inspected facilities (if available) or out of state for processing. The cost of transporting the animals, combined with animal welfare implications, has made the enterprise wholly unsustainable. Fortunately, there are some potential solutions to this. By granting USDA certification to select state packing facilities the 2008 federal farm bill allows producers to ship across state lines and broaden their access to markets. The catch is that the certification process could be a long time coming. The USDA is short on inspectors even for existing facilities, and the effort to recover from the biggest beef recall in U.S. history will stretch the agency further. Meanwhile, another alternative is for consumers to buy sustainably raised meat through community supported agriculture (CSA). In CSA, individuals "subscribe" to a program that provides a range of products, from vegetables to meat, throughout the growing season. Members become shareholders in the farm and receive its products as a return for their investment. Most CSA farms invite members to visit and even work on the farm, allowing consumers to observe animal husbandry. In sum, consumers can encourage sustainability by advocating for and supporting the infrastructure necessary for a locally based food system.

Birds, Marine Mammals, and Wildlife

The issue of oil spills raises unique problems. Whereas in some cases our individual actions can improve animal welfare in disasters, we cannot escape our reliance on petroleum. More specifically, our actions at the gas pump cannot prevent a technological catastrophe such as a tanker accident. Reducing the amount of oil we consume is a good idea, but it will not prevent spills. The issue of oil spills raises specific issues for shipping safety, and I address some of these in Chapter 3. The Oil Pollution Act of 1990 set the United States on the path to reducing oil spills and improving spill response, and the convention known as MARPOL 73/78 did the same for international waters. The mandate to make polluters liable for the costs of clean up provides a strong disincentive to spilling. Some scholars argue that although the "polluter pays" policy has decreased the number of high volume spills, it in turn has provided a false sense of security that has decreased the ability to respond when a spill does occur.[7] The mandated phase-in to double-hulled tankers also offers some protection, but as the 2015 deadline approaches, oil companies have used every available loophole to avoid compliance. ConocoPhillips is the only company to have replaced all its vessels as of 2008.[8] Meanwhile, the national energy policy must emphasize cleaner, more efficient energy, rather than petroleum exploration and production. Besides reducing the risk of oil spills, an emphasis on cleaner, more efficient energy is our only hope to slow global climate change, which may be increasing the number and severity of natural disasters. This step will require providing incentives to corporations and individuals who develop and invest in clean energy sources. Although soaring prices provided a strong financial reason to minimize petroleum usage during 2008, global energy demands will increase regardless of price. The fate of marine birds and animals, and indeed of the entire planet, depends largely on how we power the future.

In addition to the issues of cleaner energy, the discussion of how to reduce the harm to birds and animals through exposure to oil raises the broader question of what we should do for wildlife in disasters of other kinds. With oil spills, where we are clearly at fault, some intervention is ethical, provided it follows the guidelines and procedures developed by professional rehabilitators. In most spills, rescue efforts should focus on endangered or threatened species; in others, the victims should be euthanized. As I point out in Chapter 3, when large amounts of time, labor, and money go into saving birds and animals who will soon die despite our efforts—or because of them—we have to question our motives. The discussion of what to do for afflicted birds and animals often involves politics and public relations, rather than strictly humanitarian actions. The sea otters in the *Exxon Valdez* spill are a case in point. Public outcry forced action, even though no plan was in place for the otters before the spill. Millions of dollars went into a highly publicized attempt to "rescue" a few hundred animals. Many died while being "rescued," and many others did not survive long after being released. Had the spill affected a species with a lower "cuteness" factor, thus lower on the sociozoologic scale, the pleas would not have been so loud or so frequent. Moreover, Exxon most likely would not have poured so much money into a species that would not have bolstered its public image the way the sea otters did.

The discussion of oil spills raises the larger question of what we should do for wildlife in disasters. As in a spill, the best response might often be not to step in to try to save or rescue animals. However, different species elicit different responses. For example, following record snowfall in Colorado in 2007–2008, the nightly news began showing film of desperate mule deer struggling through hard-crusted, chest-deep snow to find food. Hungry elk began pillaging farmers' haystacks. The Division of Wildlife (DOW) monitored the herds in especially hard hit areas and on January 26 reported, "Despite scientific and visual assurances that wildlife health is not seriously threatened at this time, DOW offices are being flooded with calls and e-mails from concerned citizens that want immediate action."[9] Under normal circumstances, feeding and "baiting" wild animals is prohibited, and the practice of emergency winter feeding of wildlife is highly controversial. There is concern about habituating animals to humans. Deer seem to adapt well to harsh conditions and their populations tend to rebound very quickly. Incorrect feed can cause serious gastrointestinal problems, and the crowding of animals around feeding sites can spread parasites and illness, such as chronic wasting disease, which can decimate a herd and affect it for generations. Nevertheless, despite reports that there was no serious threat to the herds, in late January, the governor asked the legislature for $1.75 million and the DOW began feeding mule deer and antelope. They also "baited" elk with hay to keep them from foraging haystacks. The *Denver Post* reported that volunteers wanting to help "overwhelmed" the DOW.[10] To understand the decision to intervene, one need only consider a few facts. Colorado is renowned for deer hunting. In 2007, the number of deer hunting licenses had been the highest in nearly a decade. The DOW claimed that, in the event of a significant die-off, the subsequent decrease in hunting would mean a loss of $14 million in revenue to communities in western Colorado. Feeding deer and other wildlife was a political response to the concerns of citizens, farmers, and hunters, not a biological necessity.

Because deer are resources for humans, they are high on the sociozoologic scale. Factor in the "Bambi" effect, and the DOW simply could not stand by and let the animals starve. In contrast, consider the case of black bears in the same state. The summer of 2007 brought unusually high numbers of black bears out of the woods looking for food. A late frost combined with dry conditions from an extended drought led to a scarcity of the berries and acorns on which the bears rely. Consequently, hungry black bears came into developments and towns. They climbed backyard fruit trees and foraged through trashcans. Some entered houses, drawn by the prospect of food. Although human-bear encounters occur regularly along the urban-wildland interface, some seasons are busier than others. During 2007, the DOW captured and euthanized a record number of bears after encounters with humans. Yet, the DOW did not undertake a feeding program along the lines of that provided to the deer. They cited numerous reasons. Bears quickly learn to associate food with humans, and therefore feeding can exacerbate the problem even for generations, as mother bears teach their cubs where to find food. Because bears are not herd animals, a feeding program that drops food in designated areas will not work. Bears will fight with one another for food. Moreover, on rare occasions, bears can attack people. Colorado has a "two strike" policy for bear incidents. The DOW traps and relocates bears after a first encounter with a person, but they relocate a bear only once. They will euthanize the bear if he or she is trapped a second time. Along with these sound behavioral reasons not to undertake a feeding program for bears, there are economic and political ones. Bear hunting does take place in Colorado, but not on the enormous scale of deer hunting. The DOW describes it as a "niche" market. Thus, feeding bears to sustain numbers sufficient for hunting is not an economic necessity for towns in bear country. Moreover, the negative publicity the DOW might receive from the consequences of its "two strike" policy would dwarf any positive effects of a feeding program. For example, during the summer of 2007, wildlife officials received angry telephone calls and critical letters appeared in local newspapers. When the *Aspen Times* ran an article on August 11, 2007, about the record number of bears "dispatched" or "euthanized," the paper titled it "The Killing Fields."

Although we can do little to make the berries and oaks more plentiful for the bears, towns and counties have attempted to reduce bears' vulnerability to the consequences of human encounters. Many communities have distributed bear-proof trashcans and informed residents about the need to clean their barbecue grills, keep pet food inside, and take other measures to keep bears away. Thus, the answer to the question of what to do for wildlife in disasters depends on the species and the situation. One goal should be to avoid causing harm to the animals through our well-intended actions.

Animals Used in Research

As for disasters in research labs, I recommend extending federal protection to all species used as research subjects. In short, the Animal Welfare Act should be amended to include birds, rats, and mice bred for research. This measure will encourage compliance with the

Three R's, which is intended to reduce the numbers of animals used in research. The National Institutes of Health (NIH) should withhold funding from facilities built in high-risk areas, such as flood plains and fault lines. As I mention in Chapter 4, animal advocates have pressured the NIH to withhold funds in the past, and the organization has ignored them or responded that it does not have the capacity to take such action. Although the bureaucratic complexities of the NIH's authority are beyond the scope of my investigation, it would seem that if the agency can grant funding it could also withhold funding. Buying more animals to live in flood-prone basements seems a misguided use of taxpayer dollars.

Some research facilities, such as the University of Texas, have learned through sad experience that however carefully conceived, disaster plans do not always hold up. Flooding can prevent staff members from reaching a facility and caring for animals. An ill-placed generator can fail. Or, as in the case of Hurricane Andrew, "concerned" citizens can take matters into their own hands and kill animals released by the event. The best and final recommendation I can make applies not only to disasters in research labs but to all kinds of disasters.

"We Never Imagined"

Each chapter of this book underscores our inability to envision "worst case" scenarios. In every disaster I studied, the accounts of the event incorporated some version of "we never imagined this would happen." Sometimes it took the form of "we never expected it would be this bad." Meanwhile, every disaster planning event I have attended and all the literature I have read sends a message to "expect the unexpected." Clearly, there are obstacles to doing so. The work of Karen Cerulo offers some insights into what these might be.[11] According to Cerulo, we tend to focus on the best to the exclusion of flaws and deficiencies. She calls this bias "positive asymmetry." For example, when Cerulo polled her students, she found that they quickly and easily described the best things that could happen to them, but when asked to imagine the worst, they came up with only vague, tentative, brief depictions. They gave precise reports of how the best would involve straight A's, lottery winnings, and career success, whereas their reports of the worst amounted simply to "getting sick," "failure," or "maybe death." Cerulo documented this "failure of imagination" in settings far beyond her classroom.[12] It characterizes a wide variety of individuals and groups. We avoid thinking about death and aging, for example, preferring to believe that science will discover cures for dreaded disease by the time we need them. We take all kinds of risks, believing that the worst will never happen to us. We drive while fatigued or while talking on a cell phone, believing that serious accidents happen only to others. Organizations, too, fall prey to the failure to envision the worst. For example, the choice by officials at NASA to overlook reports of O-ring malfunction resulted in the 1986 *Challenger* tragedy.[13]

Clearly, the failure (or unwillingness) to acknowledge negative information can have devastating consequences in disasters. For example, four years before Hurricane Katrina, a report in *Scientific American* had warned that the levees in New Orleans were inadequate.[14] In 2002, the *Times-Picayune* published a five-part series on the city's vulnerability. One article said:

> A flood from a powerful hurricane can get trapped for weeks inside the levee system. Emergency officials concede that many of the structures in the area, including newer high-rise buildings, would not survive the winds of a major storm. . . . The large size of the area at risk also makes it difficult to evacuate the million or more people who live in the area, putting tens of thousands of people at risk of dying even with improved forecasting and warnings.[15]

Another article in the series reported that "a large population of low-income residents do not own cars and would have to depend on an untested emergency public transportation system to evacuate them."[16] In 2004, the five-day "Hurricane Pam" exercise predicted the breaching of the levees, the stranding of numerous residents, and the deaths of as many as sixty thousand people, mostly by drowning. Yet, President George W. Bush appeared on *Good Morning America* on September 1, 2005, and said, "I don't think anyone could have anticipated the breach of the levees." He and numerous other officials had simply not taken well-documented problems seriously. Had they given negative information its due, perhaps they could have taken steps to reduce everyone's vulnerability to Katrina.

Positive asymmetry has cognitive and cultural roots that make it difficult to overcome. Granted, much of the time, things work out just fine, even if the best does not happen, and it is psychologically better to think on the bright side. Nevertheless, as Cerulo explains, in many cases, "we regret our inability to imagine the worst. And during such times, we bemoan our biased perceptual tendencies. . . . *If only*—probably two of the most frequently uttered words in the American lexicon."[17] The inability to envision and anticipate the worst keeps us optimistic, but it also limits our capacity to prepare. Indeed, this positive asymmetry even appears in the existing books on animals in disasters.[18] The stories and photographs of rescue efforts provide important recognition for and reminders of the work people do on behalf of animals. However, they retain the "we never imagined" perspective that limits how we think about animals and disasters. They lack the analysis I have attempted to bring to the discussion. Thus, the implications of positive asymmetry have obvious relevance for disaster research and response.

In this book, I attempt to draw attention to the negative information about the hazards to which we regularly expose animals. If we want to reduce the risks of positive asymmetry, acknowledging our blind spots brings valuable information to light that can set us on the path to more symmetrical thinking. The next step involves evaluating that information, but we face a cognitive obstacle there, too. Cerulo argues that we often envision the best and worst at opposite ends of a continuum, when in fact they may entail different outcomes altogether. To illustrate, she refers to her students who listed winning lots of money among the best and death among the worst. The best and worst are not opposites but are conceptually quite different outcomes. Often the worst remains vague or unspecified. For example, before Hurricane Katrina, a best-case scenario for animal rescuers would have meant that the storm did not make landfall, and thus no animals needed rescue. Perhaps rescue organizations would have staged outside the target region and then gone home. Although I cannot say definitively how they defined the worst, it seems clear that what occurred was not only bigger but also much different from their expectations. It involved residents forced to leave their animals behind and rescuers forcibly prevented from entering the stricken areas, putting animals in greater peril with each passing day.

All the "lessons learned" presentations that I have seen and read since the 2005 hurricane season have consistent themes. Rescuers "never imagined" that they would be prevented from entering New Orleans, that there would be so many animals, that the rescue efforts would take so long, that the flood would make existing shelters unusable, or that the effort would require so many volunteers. And what lessons are to be learned? Typically, the new message is the same as the old one: Expect the unexpected. As I struggled to reconcile "we never imagined" with the mandate to "expect the unexpected," Cerulo's work shed some light on my difficulty. Reliably anticipating worst cases requires adopting a radically new way of thinking, which Cerulo calls a "separate-but-equal" strategy.[19] It involves considering best and worst cases independently. Cognitive and cultural conventions can make this an especially difficult task but a valuable one. Indeed, it may even save many lives.

We can truly help animals in disasters by making them less vulnerable. Doing so involves rethinking our uses of animals. For example, disasters would affect fewer animals if we took an obvious step and simply used fewer of them. Research facilities need to take the Three R's seriously and truly reduce the numbers of animals in use—without redefining "animals" for their convenience. If nothing else changes, and scientists must simply use fewer animals, how will we decide who does not get a grant, a publication, or a promotion for lack of research that follows the norms? In another context, how will we determine who may have animal companions? Will it only be those who have transportation, or those who do not live on the coasts? In addition to the cognitive obstacles we face when questioning our uses of animals, there are economic, practical, selfish, and sentimental obstacles, too. Convincing people that animals deserve better treatment is easy. Convincing them of the need for real change—not just bigger cages—is much more difficult. As Matthew Scully writes, in discussions about our treatment of animals, "it is always just one step from the mainstream to the fringe. To condemn the wrong is obvious, to suggest its abolition is radical."[20]

In the 1975 movie *Jaws*, when Chief Brody (played by Roy Scheider) saw the shark for the first time, he uttered the now-famous line, "You're going to need a bigger boat." In many ways, that statement sums up the current state of affairs involving animals and disasters. The situation is more serious than we imagined. We have filled the ark; there are no bigger boats. The hopeful message of this book is that once we realize how we make animals vulnerable to disasters we can begin to question and change the practices that put them at risk.

The events I depict offer but a selective glimpse of how we endanger the animals we care for and rely on so heavily. In closing, I want to mention other situations so that they, too, might spark compassionate consideration. For example, I have not discussed what happens to animals because of our desire to look at them whenever we please. In 2002, over 150 birds and animals died when floodwaters overcame the Prague Zoo. During Katrina, 10,000 fish suffocated when the Aquarium of the Americas in New Orleans lost power. Although some argue that zoos and aquariums are themselves a "Noah's Ark" for endangered species, evidence indicates that most facilities serve purely entertainment purposes.[21] Thus, we put millions of birds, animals, and fish at risk for the most trivial of human interests. I have also not discussed war, which is currently wreaking havoc on animals of all kinds in many places on the globe. The American invasion of Baghdad left the animals in the city's zoo and the Hussein family's palaces stranded and starving.[22] Wildlife in war zones face risks from munitions, land mines, habitat destruction, and disruption of migration routes. In short, any event that affects humans is also likely to affect animals. The suffering and death of animals in extraordinary events, such as disasters, should cause us to rethink our treatment of animals under ordinary circumstances. Then, instead of getting a bigger boat, perhaps we can turn the ship around.

Notes

Introduction

1. For a discussion of the distinction between pets and companion animals, see Irvine, *If You Tame Me.*

2. Park, "Lucky Few."

3. Stormont, "Help Was Never on the Way."

4. Kinney, "'Looting' or 'Finding'?"

5. See, e.g., "Katrina Victims Blame Racism for Slow Aid," NBC News, December 6, 2005, http://www.msnbc.msn.com/id/10354221.

6. Rodríguez and Barnshaw, "Social Construction of Disasters," 222. Works in the vulnerability paradigm include Blaikie et al., *At Risk*; Bolin and Stanford, *Northridge Earthquake*; Cutter, *American Hazardscapes*; Hewitt, *Interpretations of Calamity* and *Regions of Risk*; Peacock et al., *Hurricane Andrew*; Sen, *Poverty and Famine.*

7. Tierney, "Foreshadowing Katrina."

8. Blaikie et al., *At Risk*, 9.

9. Bolin and Stanford, *Northridge Earthquake*, 42.

10. Peacock et al., *Hurricane Andrew.*

11. For a review of the literature on gender and disasters, see Fothergill, "Gender, Risk, and Disaster."

12. Klinenberg, *Heat Wave*, 179, 20–21.

13. Bolin and Stanford, *Northridge Earthquake*, 9.

14. Arluke and Sanders, *Regarding Animals*, 9. See also Kalof, *Looking at Animals*.

15. Cartmill, "Hunting and Humanity in Western Thought."

16. Darwin was one of the first to challenge the idea of a great "chain of being." Examples of contemporary challenges appear in Birke, *Feminism, Animals, and Science*; Gould, *Wonderful Life*.

17. Arluke and Sanders, *Regarding Animals*, 169.

18. For an excellent case study of the blurring of the boundary, see Baron, *Beast in the Garden*.

19. McLaughlin, *Center Says State Must Act*.

20. Jones et al., *Fact Sheet #13B*.

21. See Mallin and Corbett, "How Hurricane Attributes"; Mallin et al., "Impacts and Recovery"; Wing and Band, "Potential Impact of Flooding."

22. See Douglas, *How Institutions Think*.

23. See Holstein and Miller, *Reconsidering Social Constructionism*, 5–19; Irvine, "Problem of Unwanted Pets"; Miller and Holstein, "On the Sociology of Social Problems."

24. For NIMS documents, see the organization's home page at http://www.fema.gov/emergency/nims/nims_compliance.shtm#nimsdocument.

25. National Response Plan home page, http://www.dhs.gov/xlibrary/assets/NRP_Brochure.pdf.

26. See Beaver et al., "Report of the 2006 National Animal Disaster Summit."

27. See Irvine, "Animals in Disasters"; idem, *Animals in Disasters*.

28. Diseases that are endemic in animals but that can occur on a disastrous scale are brucellosis, classical swine fever, bluetongue, FMD, wasting diseases, scrapie, and the family of equine encephalomyelitis viruses.

29. Mort et al., "Animal Disease and Human Trauma," 142. See also Convery et al., "Death in the Wrong Place."

30. Nerlich, Hillyard, and Wright, "Stress and Stereotypes," 357. For research on farmers' concern for the welfare of animals during emergencies, see Linnabary and New, "Results of a Survey"; Linnabary et al., "Attitudinal Survey of Tennessee Beef Producers."

31. There are over two hundred such diseases currently. They include SARS, E. coli, salmonella, plague, tularemia, ebola, hantavirus, monkeypox, West Nile virus, avian influenza, and prion diseases such as bovine spongiform encephalopathy (suspected to cause variant Creutzfeldt-Jakob disease in humans).

32. World Health Organization, *Emerging Zoonoses*, http://www.who.int/zoonoses/emerging_zoonoses/en/.

33. In October 2006, the World Organization for Animal Health (Office of International Epizooties) listed over twenty multispecies diseases for live-

stock, with approximately fifteen unique to cattle and sheep and seven to swine.

34. Francione, *Introduction to Animal Rights*, 153.

35. This definition comes from Dawkins, "User's Guide."

Chapter 1

1. Hayes, *Sad and Emotional Day*; Jones, "TV Show Features Ike Pet."

2. For a description of the course of the storm, including damage report, see Knabb, Rhome, and Brown, *Tropical Cyclone Report*.

3. Irvine, *Providing for Pets during Disasters: An Exploratory Study*.

4. Louisiana SPCA, *Shelter Closing; Animals Are Being Moved as Katrina Approaches* (press release, August 27, 2005), http://www.la-spca.org/archive/082705katrina.htm.

5. Leben, Born, and Scott, *CU-Boulder Researchers Chart Katrina's Growth*.

6. Associated Press, "Katrina Heads for New Orleans," FoxNews.com, August 29, 2005, http://www.foxnews.com/story/0,2933,167270,00.html.

7. Bourne, "Gone with the Water."

8. Olsen, "City Had Evacuation Plan."

9. Kaiser Family Foundation/Washington Post/Harvard University, *ICR/Kaiser/Washington Post/Harvard Poll # 2005 WPH020: Hurricane Katrina Evacuees Survey*, available at http://www.stanford.edu/group/ssds/mt-files/docs/roper/2006_aug.pdf.

10. "New Orleans Braces for Monster Hurricane," CNN.com, August 29, 2005, http://www.cnn.com/2005/WEATHER/08/28/hurricane.katrina/.

11. Foster, *Superdome Evacuations Enter Second Day*.

12. Haygood and Tyson, "It Was as if All of Us."

13. Dauphin, *There's Something about Lily*. Incredibly, Lily was reunited with the Menendezes, who relocated to Fort Smith, Arkansas.

14. Best Friends Network, *Update: St. Bernard School Shootings*, February 4, 2006, http://network.bestfriends.org/hurricane/news/1741.html.

15. For Anderson Cooper's coverage of the dogs killed at the evacuation center, see http://www.cnn.com/video/player/player.html?url=/video/us/2005/09/30/cooper.dogs.shot.cnn. Additional footage of the shootings is on YouTube; see http://www.youtube.com/watch?v=KtU2AFCbJlY.

16. Scott, "Update."

17. Anderson and Anderson, *Rescued*, 42–43.

18. The staging area for the Mississippi animal response was located in Hattiesburg.

19. The students of the Louisiana State University School of Veterinary Medicine's large animal program cared for the 350 horses also housed at Lamar-Dixon.

20. Michelle Davis, *Faces of Katrina*, http://www.pitbullsontheweb.com/petbull/katrina.php.

21. *Animal Protection Organizations Urge Shelters and Rescue Groups with Katrina Pets to Extend Holding Time*, Louisiana SPCA press release, October 12, 2005, http://www.la-spca.org/archive/101205requestb.htm.

22. For more information about Maddie's Fund, see the organization's home page at http://www.maddiesfund.org/index.html.

23. The PETS Act became Public Law 109-308.

24. For a report on the memorial service, see *Memorial Honors Katrina Animals*, Louisiana SPCA press release, August 8, 2006, http://www.la-spca.org/archive/memorial080806.htm.

25. American Veterinary Medical Association, *U.S. Pet Ownership*, 1–3.

26. Loseke, *Thinking about Social Problems*, 75–95.

27. See, e.g., Heath et al., "Risk Factors for Pet Evacuation Failure"; Heath et al., "Epidemiological Study of Cats and Dogs." These factors were similar to those associated with surrender to a shelter in nondisaster settings. See Salman et al., "Human and Animal Factors."

28. Heath et al., "Human and Pet Related Risk Factors," 661; see also Dynes, "Disaster Event and Community Stress"; Peny, Lindell, and Greene, "Evacuation Experiences."

29. For a report on the temporary sheltering of animals with confirmed guardians, see "LSU Responds to Care for Animals in the Aftermath of Hurricanes Katrina and Rita," *La veterinaire*, October 2005, http://www.vetmed.lsu.edu/Web_pdfs/October05LaVet.pdf.

30. Heath, "Human and Pet Related Risk Factors," 664.

31. Ibid.

32. Further information about increased numbers of animals at shelters appears in Irvine, *Providing for Pets during Disasters, Part II*.

33. Heath et al., "Human and Pet Related Risk Factors," 664.

34. Heath and Champion, "Human Health Concerns," 69.

35. See Heath, Voeks, and Glickman, "Epidemiological Features of Pet Evacuation Failure."

Chapter 2

1. U.S. Department of Agriculture, *Livestock Slaughter*; idem, *Poultry Slaughter*.

2. Lawrence, "Neoteny in American Perceptions of Animals," 46.

3. Serpell, *In the Company of Animals*, 5.

4. For more on the transformation of agriculture, see, e.g., Bowler, "Industrialization of Agriculture"; Lobao and Meyer, "Great Agricultural Transition"; Molnar, Hobart, and Bryant, "Passing the Cluck."

5. Beaver et al., "Report of the 2006 National Animal Disaster Summit."

6. These issues are part of a research agenda proposed by Plous, "Psychological Mechanisms."

7. West and Zhou, "Did Chickens Go North?"; Glatz, Critchley, and Lunam, "Domestic Chicken."

8. Molnar, Hoban, and Bryant, "Passing the Cluck"; Sambidi, Harrison, and Farr, *Conjoint Analysis of Site Selection*, 3.

9. Ernst, *Poultry Fact Sheet No. 20*; Orlans et al., *Human Use of Animals*, 256.

10. Sambidi, Harrison, and Farr, *Conjoint Analysis of Site Selection*, 3. According to the U.S. Poultry and Egg Association, the top ten broiler producers are Tyson Foods, Pilgrim's Pride Corporation, Gold Kist, Perdue Farms Inc., Sanderson Farms, Wayne Farms LLC., Mountaire Farms Inc., Foster Farms, OK Foods Inc., and Peco Foods Inc.

11. Molnar, Hoban, and Bryant, "Passing the Cluck," 91.

12. According to the USDA's National Agricultural Statistics Service, the precise figures for 2004 egg production, the most recent available, is 343 million laying hens.

13. United Egg Producers, *United Egg Producers Animal Husbandry Guidelines*.

14. Franklin, *Animals and Modern Cultures*, 137.

15. Cody, "Tyson Shifting Its Ports on Gulf."

16. "Sanderson Farms, Inc. Provides Update on Hurricane Katrina Damage," *Investor Relations Overview: News Release*, September 6, 2005, http://phx.corporate-ir.net/phoenix.zhtml?c=68801&p=irol-newsArticle&ID=753218&highlight=.

17. All quotations from Kate Walker and Kim Sturla in this chapter, unless otherwise attributed, are from interviews by the author, February 7, 2007.

18. Articles on the Buckeye rescue are available from the Farm Sanctuary home page at http://www.farmsanctuary.org/. On the company's environmental record, see Natural Resources Defense Council, *America's Animal Factories: How States Fail to Prevent Pollution from Livestock Waste*, http://www.nrdc.org/water/pollution/factor/stohi.asp; EggCruelty.com, *Dirty Histories: A History of Buckeye Egg Farm*, http://www.eggcruelty.com/dirtyhistories.asp.

19. In 2003, the Ohio Department of Agriculture ordered Buckeye Egg Farm to cease production because of numerous pollution and nuisance violations dating to 1997. In 2004, Buckeye was sold to another company, Ohio Fresh Eggs. The new owners have also been cited for environmental and OSHA violations.

20. Quoted in Erik Markus, *Buckeye: The Shelter Movement's Finest Hour*, http://www.vegsource.com/articles/buckeye.htm.

21. Quoted in Farm Sanctuary's account of the rescue, retrieved February 6, 2007, from http://www.farmsanctuary.org/newsletter/disaster.htm.

22. All quotations from Susie Coston in this chapter are from an interview by the author, February 7, 2007. Poultry science scholars agree that carrying birds upright, rather than by the feet, which is standard practice on chicken farms, leads to less stress among the birds. See, e.g., Kannan and Mench, "Influence of Different Handling Methods."

23. Quoted in Mark Williams, *Residents Adopt Tornado Chickens*, http://www.upc-online.org/buckeye_egg_farm.html.

24. Singer, *Animal Liberation*. Farmed animals also appear in documentaries less often than wildlife and companion animals do.

25. Adams, *Sexual Politics of Meat*. See also Plous, "Psychological Mechanisms."

26. Walsh, "1,000 Chickens."

27. Herzog, Rowan, and Kassow, "Social Attitudes to Animals."

28. Norwood, Lusk, and Prickett, *Consumer Preferences for Farm Animal Welfare*, 17.

29. Pew Commission, *Putting Meat on the Table*, 23.

30. Steinfeld et al., *Livestock's Long Shadow*, 79–123.

31. Pew Commission, *Putting Meat on the Table*, 85.

32. Ibid.

33. For a description of hoop barns for pigs and a summary of research on productivity, see Iowa State University, College of Agriculture, *Hoop Barn Swine Production*, http://www.leopold.iastate.edu/pubs/other/files/hoopsheet.pdf.

34. Pew Commission, *Putting Meat on the Table*, 85.

35. International Working Group on Animals in Disasters, *Protecting Animals from Disasters*, 1.

36. Leslie and Sunstein, "Animal Rights without Controversy," 133–134. The authors present a thorough discussion of the disclosure of the treatment of animals used for food.

37. Humane Research Council, *Advocating Meat Reduction*, 5–7.

38. *"Act of God" Exposes Egg Industry's Body and Soul: Another Reason to Boycott the Egg Industry*, Vegan Outreach, http://www.veganoutreach.org/eggs/.

Chapter 3

1. Hartley made the statement about "a few birds" in Senate Subcommittee on Air and Water Pollution, *Amendments to the Federal Water Pollution Control Act—Hearings* (91st Cong., 1st sess.), February 5, 1969. For accounts of the impact of these hearings, including Hartley's statement, see Clarke and Hemphill, "Santa Barbara Oil Spill," 159; Weaver, "Senate Hearing Held," 1969.

2. See Birkland, "In the Wake of the *Exxon Valdez*."

3. The number of birds is an underestimate, based only on recovered carcasses. It does not include birds whose bodies did not reach the shore. Carter, "Oil and California's Seabirds," 2. See also Clarke and Hemphill, "Santa Barbara Oil Spill"; McCrary, Panzer, and Pierson, "Oil and Gas Operations Offshore California."

4. Santa Barbara Wildlife Care Network, *Santa Barbara's 1969 Oil Spill*, http://www.sbwcn.org/spill.shtml.

5. National Research Council, *Oil in the Sea*.

6. The International Tanker Owners Pollution Federation, Ltd., maintains a database of spills at http://www.itopf.com/information-services/data-and-statistics/.

7. For a few examples of the large literature on the impact of the *Exxon Valdez* spill on birds, see Fry, "How Do You Fix the Loss of Half a Million Birds?"; Piatt and Ford, "How Many Seabirds Were Killed?"; Piatt and Lensink, "*Exxon Valdez* Bird Toll"; Piatt et al., "Immediate Impact of the 'Exxon Valdez' Oil Spill." For the *Erika* spill, see Ridoux et al., "Impact of the 'Erika' Oil Spill." For rescue efforts following the sinking of the *MV Treasure*, see IBRRC, *20,000 Patient Penguins*. On the *Prestige* spill, see Vince, "Prestige Oil Spill"; Kirby, "Spanish Spill Not Over Yet"; IBRRC, *New Year*. The *Prestige* spilled more oil than the *Exxon Valdez* did, and the oil had a higher toxicity level; the oil and water were also at a higher temperature, making it spread more quickly.

8. García-Borboroglu et al., "Chronic Oil Pollution Harms Magellanic Penguins," 193.

9. For a thorough examination of sources of marine oil pollution, see National Research Council, *Oil in the Sea*.

10. Boersma,"Penguins Oiled in Argentina"; Gandini et al., "Magellanic Penguins Affected by Chronic Petroleum Pollution"; Heredia et al., "Evolution of Penguin Rehabilitation"; Jehl, "Mortality of Magellanic Penguins"; Ruoppolo et al., *Chronic Oiling*; Ruoppolo et al., "Update on the IFAW Penguin Network."

11. For a report on the impact of the unidentified spill, see "Davis Experts Say Oil Spill Is World's Worst for Birds since 2002," *Science News*, January 24, 2005, http://www.sciencedaily.com/releases/2005/01/050121105359.htm.

12. National Research Council, *Oil in the Sea*, 67–70.

13. Santa Barbara Wildlife Care Network, *Cleaning Oiled Birds*, http://www.sbwcn.org/oiled.shtml.

14. Weaver, "Senate Hearing Held"; "Environment: Tragedy in Oil," *Time.com*, February 14, 1969, http://www.time.com/time/magazine/article/0,9171,900613-3,00.html.

15. Public Law 91-190, 42 U.S.C. 4321-4347, January 1, 1970.

16. For a concise history of the Environmental Protection Agency, see Jack Lewis, "The Birth of EPA," *EPA Journal*, November 1985, http://www.epa.

gov/history/topics/epa/15c.htm. Historical documents relating to Earth Day are available at http://www.epa.gov/history/topics/earthday/index.htm.

17. Franklin, *Animals and Modern Cultures*, 59.

18. Abraham Gesner, a Canadian medical doctor with a keen interest in geology, first distilled kerosene from crude oil in 1846. He reportedly said that he hoped the new oil would end the killing of whales. In 1851, James Young, a Scotsman, produced kerosene by distilling it from coal and oil shale.

19. In January 1999 the global oil tanker fleet numbered 7,030. Commission on the European Communities, *Communication from the Commission to the European Parliament*.

20. By 1955, two-thirds of the world's oil moved through the Suez Canal, accounting for half of its traffic. Yergin, *Prize*, 464.

21. Daniel Ludwig, known as the father of jumboization, purportedly said that the only limit on tanker size is the size of the ocean. Potter, *Disaster by Oil*, 6 (see chap. 6 for a discussion of jumboization).

22. Known as "aframax," for "average freight rate assessment," the sizing system was developed by Shell Oil in 1954 to standardize shipping rates. See Von Sydow, "Sizing Up the Bulk Sector."

23. Crude oil is traded in lots of five hundred thousand barrels. For perspective, the United States consumes approximately twenty million barrels a day. (These are not literal barrels; *barrel* refers to a unit of volume.)

24. Cowan, *Oil and Water*, 11. For a detailed history of the *Torrey Canyon* incident, see Potter, *Disaster by Oil*, chap. 1.

25. Cowan, *Oil and Water*, 223.

26. Potter, *Disaster by Oil*, 28.

27. Ott, *Sound Truths*, 10.

28. For a discussion of how the *Torrey Canyon* incident raised concerns about existing measures to prevent oil pollution, see *International Convention for the Prevention of Pollution from Ships, 1973, as modified by the Protocol of 1978 relating thereto (MARPOL)*, http://www.imo.org/Conventions/mainframe. asp?topic_id=258&doc_id=678#4.

29. Cowan, *Oil and Water*, 157.

30. Figures are from the Royal Society for the Prevention of Cruelty to Animals, quoted in Cowan, *Oil and Water*, 160. See also National Oceanic and Atmospheric Administration, *Oil Spill Case Histories*, 195.

31. For a discussion of the effects of oil on birds, see International Bird Rescue Research Center, *How Oil Affects Birds*, http://www.ibrrc.org/oil_affects. html.

32. Erasmus, Randall, and Randall, "Oil Pollution, Insulation, and Body Temperatures in the Jackass Penguin"; Miller and Welte, "Caring for Oiled Birds."

33. For a history of the spill and response, see Santa Barbara Wildlife Care Network, *Santa Barbara's 1969 Oil Spill*, http://www.sbwcn.org/spill.shtml.

34. International Petroleum Industry Environmental Conservation Association, *Guide to Oiled Wildlife Response Planning*, 7.

35. Heubeck et al., "Assessing the Impact of Major Oil Spills," 900.

36. See Berkner, "Wildlife Rehabilitation Techniques"; Newman et al., "Historical Account of Oiled Wildlife Care."

37. Standard Oil later became Chevron.

38. Carter, "Oil and California's Seabirds." For details on the numbers of birds treated and released after oil spills in California between 1971 and 1979, see International Bird Rescue Research Center, *Spill History: 1971–79*, http://www.ibrrc.org/spill_history_1971-79.html.

39. All quotations from Alice Berkner, unless otherwise attributed, are from Berkner, *Genesis of IBRRC.*

40. IBRRC, "Founder Alice Berkner Reflects."

41. Reid, Battaglia, and Doucette, "Review of Factors," 146.

42. The American Petroleum Institute provided grant money for comparative research on solvents and detergents. See Bryndza et al., "Methodology for Determining Surfactant Efficacy."

43. IBRRC, "35 Years of Advancing Aquatic Bird Rehabilitation," 6.

44. Exxon's figure is 10.8 million gallons, putting the *Exxon Valdez* spill at number thirty among the top sixty-five spills worldwide. Other calculations put the volume between 27 and 38 million gallons, bringing it to number fifteen. The state of Alaska surveyors report a conservative estimate of 30 million gallons. The debate is chronicled in Ott, *Sound Truths*, 4–7.

45. The *Exxon Valdez* Oil Spill Trustee Council explains how the *Exxon Valdez* ran aground and provides answers to other questions related to the spill in *Oil Spill Facts: Questions and Answers*, http://www.evostc.state.ak.us/facts/qanda.cfm.

46. For more on injury to mammals and birds, see Dahlheim and Matkin, "Assessment of Injuries to Prince William Sound Orcas"; Irons et al., "Nine Years after the *Exxon Valdez* Oil Spill," 724; Mearns, "*Exxon Valdez* Shoreline Treatment and Operations." For a summary of injury to animals, see "After the *Exxon Valdez* Oil Spill," *Alaska's Marine Resources*, October 1992, http://seagrant.uaf.edu/bookstore/pubs/QTR-VII-3.pdf.

47. Bodkin and Weltz, "Evaluation of Sea Otter Capture," 65.

48. Batten, "Press Interest in Sea Otters," 32.

49. Bukro, "U.S. Bureaucracy Halts Rescuers."

50. Batten, "Press Interest in Sea Otters," 33, 37.

51. Sharp, "Post Release Survival." See also Mead, "Cleaned but Not Saved?"

52. Anderson, Gress, and Fry, "Survival and Dispersal of Oiled Brown Pelicans," 717.

53. Mead, "Poor Prospects for Oiled Birds."

54. Estes, "Catastrophes and Conservation."

55. IBRRC, *Frequently Asked Questions,* http://www.ibrrc.org/faq.html.

56. U.S. Energy Information Administration data on all energy sources are available at http://www.eia.doe.gov/fuelrenewable.html.

57. Peregrine Systems, *The Birdadvert System,* http://www.birdavert.com/. For further descriptions of deterrence systems, see Ronconi et al., "Waterbird Deterrence at Oil Spills"; Sharp, "Chasing Birds from Oil Spills"; Whisson and Takekawa, *Testing the Effectiveness.*

58. The International Maritime Organization is an agency of the United Nations. The treaties are the 1973 International Convention for the Prevention of Pollution from Ships, referred to as the MARPOL Protocol (MARPOL stands for "marine pollution") and the Protocol of 1978 relating to the International Convention for the Prevention of Pollution from Ships. The two treaties are known as MARPOL 73/78. Over 95 percent of the global shipping tonnage is transported under the flags of MARPOL signatories. MARPOL also covers garbage, sewage, and other hazardous substances.

59. Commission on the European Communities, *Communication from the Commission to the European Parliament,* 18.

60. Tippee, "Prestige Spill Raises Questions of Accountability," 68.

61. The Oil Pollution Act of 1990 (33 U.S.C. 2701-2761) gives the U.S. Coast Guard the authority to respond to marine oil spills and empowers the federal government to direct all spill responses. The act, which created the Oil Spill Liability Trust Fund, requires coastal areas to develop contingency plans for oil spills and tanker owners to create oil spill response plans. Also it increased penalties for noncompliance and authorizes each state to establish its own laws regarding liability.

62. Ramseur, *Oil Spills in U.S. Coastal Waters,* 12.

63. Fulton, "Big Oil Plays a Dirty Game."

64. See the testimony of Tom Godfrey, chair of the Shipbuilders Council of America, before the Senate Commerce, Science, and Transportation Committee, January 9, 2003, at http://commerce.senate.gov/pdf/godfrey010903.pdf.

Chapter 4

1. Lim, "Research Monkeys Fall Victim."

2. See Perrow, *Next Catastrophe,* 1 n.1.

3. For the Ohio State University incident, see Associated Press, *Nearly 700 Lab Animals Die after Power Outage,* http://www.msnbc.msn.com/

id/13880104/. For the Wyeth incident, see Ginsberg, "Lab Mice Meet Untimely Demise." For the NIH facility, see Specter, "Lab Mishap Destroys AIDS Mice."

4. See Orlans, "Data on Animal Experimentation"; Carbone, *What Animals Want*. Although the total number of animals used in research is staggering, it is still less than 1 percent of the number of animals killed for food.

5. For a discussion of the identification of animals as "heroes" and the use of the term *sacrifice*, see Arluke, "Sacrificial Symbolism in Animal Experimentation"; Birke, Arluke, and Michael, *Sacrifice*, 69, 100; Lynch, "Sacrifice and the Transformation of the Animal Body"; Phillips, "Proper Names."

6. Risk Management Solutions, *Tropical Storm Allison*, 6, 8; Berger, "Med Center Warned on Flooding in '99."

7. In its path from the Gulf region to the mid-Atlantic states, Allison took close to fifty human lives.

8. Schub, "Year of the Flood," 35, 36; Risk Management Solutions, *Tropical Storm Allison*, 11. For the Baylor College of Medicine's account of the flood, see "Dr. Feigin Reports on Flood Damage and Recovery," *Portal*, Fall 2001. Available at http://connect.bcm.edu/Page.aspx?pid=403.

9. Quoted in Schub, "Year of the Flood," 8.

10. Aronauer, "Animal-Rights Groups Demand Punishment."

11. Berger, "Lab Animals Drown."

12. Aynesworth, "Floods Ruin Years of Health Research."

13. Berger, "'We Failed Them.'"

14. Goodwin, *Water, Water: Everywhere*.

15. Quoted in Brown, "New Space," 14.

16. On the labels we assign to rodents, see Herzog, "Conflicts of Interest"; idem, "Human Morality and Animal Research; Birke, "Who—or What—Are the Rats?"

17. Herzog, "Moral Status of Mice," 473. On the moral status we attribute to animals, see also Burghardt and Herzog, "Beyond Conspecifics."

18. On the breeding of dogs and cats, see Ritvo, *Animal Estate*, 84–85, 93–94, 115–121. On the creation of animals, especially mice, standardized for research, see Birke, "Who—or What—Are the Rats?"; Maher, "Test Tubes with Tails"; Rader, *Making Mice*, chaps. 1–3; Rader, "Mouse People"; Birke, Arluke, and Michael, *Sacrifice*, chap. 1.

19. The political and cultural efforts to define cancer as a social problem worthy of research and philanthropy have received significant scholarly attention. See, e.g., Patterson, *Dread Disease*, chaps. 1, 3, 5, 7; Fujimora, *Crafting Science*, 6.

20. Rader, "Multiple Meanings of Laboratory Animals," 393–394.

21. Ahern, "Rodent Revolution."

22. Genetic material from bioluminescent jellyfish is frequently inserted into mice so that particular genes will illuminate when activated.

23. For concise histories of the industrial production of rodents, see Rader, *Making Mice*, chaps. 1–3; "Staats, "Laboratory Mouse." For lists of the many strains of rodents available for sale, see the home pages of Jackson Laboratories (http://jaxmice.jax.org/index.html), Charles River Labs (http://www.criver.com/index.html), and Taconic Farms (http://www.taconic.com).

24. On the standardization of animals for laboratory research, see Arluke, "We Build a Better Beagle"; Birke, "Who—or What—Are the Rats?"; Birke, Arluke, and Michael, *Sacrifice*, esp. chap. 1; Logan, "Before There Were Standards."

25. Birke, Arluke, and Michael, *Sacrifice*, 27; Maher, "Test Tubes with Tails."

26. Logan, "Before There Were Standards," 355.

27. LaFollette and Shanks, *Brute Science*, 19.

28. See ibid., esp. chap. 4, for a thorough discussion of causal analogical models. On the adoption of animal models of human behavior in psychology, see Shapiro, "Rodent for Your Thoughts."

29. LaFollette and Shanks, *Brute Science*, 63.

30. For discussions of the culture of science and the training of scientists, see Birke, Arluke, and Michael, *Sacrifice*, esp. chap 2. See also Latour and Woolgar, *Laboratory Life*, chaps. 1–2; Knorr-Cetina, *Epistemic Cultures*, chaps. 1, 2, 9.

31. American Medical Association, *Statement on the Use of Animals in Biomedical Research*; Sigma Xi, "Sigma Xi Statement of the Use of Animals in Research."

32. For justifications of the use of animals in research, see LaFollette and Shanks, *Brute Science*, esp. chap. 1; Arluke, "Ethical Socialization of Animal Researchers."

33. Phinizy, "Lost Pets That Stray to the Lab."

34. Wayman, "Concentration Camps for Lost and Stolen Pets."

35. Public Law 89-544, 80 Stat. 352 (1966), sec. 13, http://www.nal.usda.gov/awic/legislat/pl89544.htm. The government agency responsible for enforcing the Animal Welfare Act is the Animal Care Program of the Animal and Plant Health Inspection Service of the United States Department of Agriculture.

36. Public Law 91-579, Animal Welfare Act of 1970, 91st Cong., H.R. 19846, December 24, 1970, http://www.nal.usda.gov/awic/legislat/pl91579.htm. For a discussion of the injustice of excluding mice and rats, while including gerbils and guinea pigs, see Orlans, "Injustice of Excluding Laboratory Rats, Mice, and Birds."

37. Department of Agriculture, Animal and Plant Health Inspection Service, 9 CFR Parts 2 and 3 [Docket No. 98–106–4], *Summary*, http://www.nal.usda.gov/awic/pubs/AWA2007/04-12785.pdf.

38. For a discussion of how species determines the treatment of animals in the lab, see Carbone, *What Animals Want*, chap. 4.

39. The Three R's were originally proposed in 1954 by Charles Hume of the Universities Federation for Animal Welfare. A task force on humane treatment of animals in research was formed. William Russell, a zoologist, and Rex Burch, a microbiologist, were appointed to study humane experimental techniques. Their work produced the 1959 volume *Principles of Humane Experimental Technique*.

40. For the 1985 revisions, see Public Law 99-198 Food Security Act of 1985, Subtitle F, Animal Welfare, Dec. 23, 1985, Food Security Act of 1985, Title XVII-Related and Miscellaneous Matters, http://www.nal.usda.gov/awic/legislat/pl99198.htm.

41. For the NIH standards for animal care and use in laboratories, see Institute for Laboratory Animal Research, *Guide for the Care and Use of Laboratory Animals*.

42. The NIH relies on written assurances from funded institutions that they are complying with standards for the acquisition and welfare of animals. Research facilities can provide evidence of compliance by obtaining accreditation from the Association for Assessment and Accreditation of Laboratory Animal Care. This private accrediting agency receives no public scrutiny and site visit reports are confidential, in contrast to the U.S. Department of Agriculture's reports on Animal Welfare Act violations, which are publicly available government documents. For a thorough examination of the differences between the Animal Welfare Act and the NIH guidelines, see Carbone, *What Animals Want*, chap. 2.

43. The NIH did not respond to several inquiries about the proportion of funding provided to experiments on animals.

44. Carbone points out that in many settings, animals have no federal welfare protection. Although mice, rats, and birds are exempt from the Animal Welfare Act, their care is regulated through NIH guidelines. However, these guidelines apply only in federally funded research. Thus, facilities receiving no federal funding and using only mice and rats bred for research are exempt from regulation. Ibid.

45. Capaldo's letter to the *Houston Chronicle*, dated October 16, 2001, is posted at http://www.neavs.org/programs/avoiceforanimals/lte_houston_chronicle_10162001.htm.

46. PETA's request to the NIH, dated September 22, 2005, is posted at http://www.peta.org/mc/NewsItem.asp?id=7134.

47. PETA sent two letters to Johanns, on September 1 and 15, 2005. The first asks him to follow up on the status of the monkeys and apes in research facilities at Tulane. The second, sent after the group learned about the deaths of the LSU animals, calls for sanctions. The letters are posted at http://

stopanimaltests.com/pdfs/2005-09-01_LetterUSDAAnimalsafterKatrina.pdf; andhttp://stopanimaltests.com/pdfs/2005-09-15_LetterUSDA_LSU_HurricaneKatrina. pdf. PETA's letter to Mike Leavitt, dated September 15, 2005, is posted at http:// stopanimaltests.com/pdf/91505LetterLeavitt_LSU_Katrina.pdf. PETA's letter to LSU chancellor John Rock, dated September 16, 2005, is posted at http:// stopanimaltests.com/pdf/91605Letter%20to%20Chancellor_LSU_re%20Katrina. pdf. For PETA's letter to LSU chancellor John Rock, dated September 16, 2005, see http://stopanimaltests.com/pdf/91605Letter%20to%20Chancellor_LSU_ re%20Katrina.pdf.

48. Office of Laboratory Animal Welfare (OLAW), Office of Extramural Research, "Guidance on Prompt Reporting to OLAW under the PHS [Public Health Service] Policy on Humane Care and Use of Laboratory Animals," http://grants.nih.gov/grants/guide/notice-files/NOT-OD-05-034.html.

49. Gluck and Kubacki, "Animals in Biomedical Research," 160.

50. LaFollette and Shanks, *Brute Science*, chap. 1.

51. Analysis by McKinlay and McKinlay indicates that the "introduction of specific medical measures & expansion of services account for only a fraction of the decline in mortality since 1900." "The Questionable Contribution of Medical Measures," 405. See also McKinlay, McKinlay, and Beaglehole, "Review of the Evidence."

52. Kieswer, "PCRM Urges Texas Medical Center." See also the PCRM news release, dated June 15, 2001, urging the NIH and the Texas Medical Center not to replace the drowned animals: *Physicians Oppose Replacing Drowned Animals in Texas Labs,* http://www.pcrm.org/news/issues010615.html.

53. LaFollette and Shanks, *Brute Science*, chaps. 2, 16; Pound et al., "Where Is the Evidence?"

54. Roberts et al., "Does Animal Experimentation Inform Human Healthcare?"

55. Hackam and Redelmeier, "Translation of Research Evidence." See also Perel et al., "Comparison of Treatment Effects," which reports that "discordance between animal and human studies may be due to bias or to the failure of animal models to mimic clinical disease adequately" (197).

56. Vioxx, a Cox-2 drug (such drugs target the cyclooxygenase-2 enzyme involved in inflammation and associated pain), was associated with more deaths than any medication to that point—and more Americans died from taking it than died in the Vietnam War. Another cox-2 drug, Bextra, was also withdrawn when it was shown to produce excess deaths in surgical patients, and another, Celebrex, has never been withdrawn, but it received a black-box warning in 2005 regarding the risks for cardiovascular thrombosis and gastrointestinal bleeding. It is the only cox-2 drug currently approved by the U.S. Food and Drug Administration.

57. A review of the vast literature on animal welfare and animal rights is beyond the scope of this chapter. I refer readers to Singer, *Animal Liberation*; Regan, *Case for Animal Rights*; Francione, *Introduction to Animal Rights*; and Wise, *Rattling the Cage*.

58. The term *speciesism* originated in Ryder, *Victims of Science*.

59. Gluck and Kubacki, "Animals in Biomedical Research," 158.

60. Groves, *Hearts and Minds*, chaps. 4–6.

61. This agreement is illustrated by acceptance of the Three R's. See Rudacille, *Scalpel and the Butterfly*, 268–269; DeGrazia, "Ethics of Animal Research."

62. Carbone, *What Animals Want*, 239.

63. Ibrahim, *Reduce, Refine, Replace*.

64. Carbone, *What Animals Want*, 3.

65. Plous and Herzog, "Poll Shows Researchers Favor Lab Animal Protection"; idem, "Should the Animal Welfare Act Cover Rats, Mice, and Birds?" See also Rudacille, *Scalpel and the Butterfly*, 301–313.

66. For a discussion of the loopholes researchers can employ to avoid compliance with the Three R's, see Ibrahim, *Reduce, Refine, Replace*.

67. For full discussions of regulating lab work, see Birke, Arluke, and Michael, *Sacrifice*, chap. 6; Greek and Greek, *Sacred Cows and Golden Geese*, chap. 5.

68. Pound et al., "Where Is the Evidence?" 516. See also Smith, "Comroe and Dripps Revisited."

Conclusion

1. See Irvine, "Animals in Disasters."

2. Perrow, *Next Catastrophe*, 66.

3. Starmer and Wise, *Feeding at the Trough* estimates that subsidized feed saved agribusiness $3.9 billion a year for the eight-year-period analyzed, or $35 billion overall.

4. Wise, "Identifying the Real Winners."

5. Michael Pollan, "The Farm Bill: What Went Wrong," posted June 4, 2008, at *Grist: Environmental News and Commentary*, http://gristmill.grist.org/story/2008/6/4/43736/55179.

6. Pew Commission, *Putting Meat on the Table*, 75.

7. See, e.g., Ramseur, *Oil Spills in U.S. Coastal Waters*.

8. At the same time, the Sierra Club gives ConocoPhillips "at the bottom of the barrel" environmental rankings. For the rankings of major oil companies, see Sarah Ives and Robynne Boyd, "Pick Your Poison," *Sierra*, January/February 2007, http://www.sierraclub.org/sierra/pickyourpoison/#conoco.

9. DOW, *DOW Monitoring Winter Conditions in Northwest Colorado*, January 25, 2008, http://dnr.state.co.us/newsapp/press.asp?pressid=4732.

10. Howard Pankratz, *Denver Post*, http://www.denverpost.com/ci_7999570?source=rss.

11. Cerulo, *Never Saw It Coming*.

12. The term *failure of imagination* attained mainstream currency in commentaries following the 9/11 attacks. See ibid., 18–20.

13. See, e.g., Vaughan, *Challenger Launch Decision*, xii, xiv.

14. Fischetti, "Drowning New Orleans."

15. McQuaid and Schleifstein, "In Harm's Way."

16. McQuaid and Schleifstein, "Left Behind."

17. Cerulo, *Never Saw It Coming*, 233; emphasis added.

18. See, for example, Anderson and Anderson, *Rescued*; Best Friends Animal Society, *Not Left Behind*; Crisp and Glen, *Out of Harm's Way*; Crisp, *Emergency Animal Rescue Stories*; Heath, *Animal Management in Disasters*; Heath and O'Shea, *Rescuing Rover*.

19. Cerulo, *Never Saw It Coming*, 239–242.

20. Scully, *Dominion*, 351.

21. Jamieson, "Against Zoos."

22. Anthony, *Babylon's Ark*, esp. chaps. 2–6.

Bibliography

Adams, Carol. *The Sexual Politics of Meat: A Feminist Vegetarian Critical Theory.* 10th Anniversary Edition. New York: Continuum, 1999.

Ahern, Holly. "The Rodent Revolution." *Scientist* 9 (1995): 18.

Allan, Carrie. *Refusing to Leave Them Behind, Evacuees Smuggled Their Pets Out with Them.* Humane Society of the United States, September 4, 2005. Available at http://www.hsus.org/hsus_field/hsus_disaster_center/disasters_press_room/archives/.

American Medical Association. *Statement on the Use of Animals in Biomedical Research.* Chicago: American Medical Association, 1992.

American Veterinary Medical Association. *U.S. Pet Ownership and Demographics Sourcebook.* Schaumburg, IL: Center for Information Management of the American Veterinary Medical Association, 2007.

Anderson, Allen, and Linda Anderson. *Rescued: Saving Animals from Disaster.* Novato, CA: New World Library, 2006.

Anderson, Daniel W., Franklin Gress, and D. Michael Fry. "Survival and Dispersal of Oiled Brown Pelicans after Rehabilitation and Release." *Marine Pollution Bulletin* 32 (1996): 711–718.

Anthony, Lawrence. *Babylon's Ark: The Incredible Wartime Rescue of the Baghdad Zoo.* New York: St. Martin's, 2007.

Arluke, Arnold. "The Ethical Socialization of Animal Researchers." *Lab Animal* 23 (1994): 30–35.

———. "Sacrificial Symbolism in Animal Experimentation: Object or Pet?" *Anthrozoös* 2 (1988): 97–116.

———. "'We Build a Better Beagle': Fantastic Creatures in Lab Animal Ads." *Qualitative Sociology* 17 (1994): 143–157.

Arluke, Arnold, and Clinton R. Sanders. *Regarding Animals*. Philadelphia: Temple University Press, 1996.

Aronauer, Rebecca. "Animal-Rights Groups Demand Punishment for LSU over Lab Animals' Deaths." *Chronicle of Higher Education*, September 30, 2005. http://chronicle.com/free/v52/i06/06a01902.htm.

Aynesworth, Hugh. "Floods Ruin Years of Health Research; Texas Medical Center Was Inundated." *Washington Times*, June 25, 2001.

Baker, Steve. *The Postmodern Animal*. London: Reaktion Books, 2000.

Baron, David. *The Beast in the Garden: A Modern Parable of Man and Nature*. New York: Norton, 2004.

Batten, Bruce T. "Press Interest in Sea Otters Affected by the T/V *Exxon Valdez* Oil Spill: A Star Is Born." Pp. 26–40 in *Sea Otter Symposium: Proceedings of a Symposium to Evaluate the Response Effort on Behalf of Sea Otters after the T/V Exxon Valdez Oil Spill into Prince William Sound, Anchorage, Alaska*. U.S. Fish and Wildlife Service Biological Report 90. Washington, DC: U.S. Government Printing Office, 1990.

Beaver, B. V., R. Gros, E. M. Bailey, and C. S. Lovern. "Report of the 2006 National Animal Disaster Summit." *Journal of the American Veterinary Medical Association* 229 (2006): 943–948.

Bekoff, Marc. *Strolling with Our Kin: Speaking for and Respecting Voiceless Animals*. New York: Lantern Books, 2000.

Berger, Eric. "Lab Animals Drown; Medical Research Lost." *Houston Chronicle*, June 12, 2001.

———. "Med Center Warned on Flooding in '99; Project's Length, Cost Deterred Action." *Houston Chronicle*, June 14, 2001.

———. "'We Failed Them, and It's Terrible'; Drownings of 78 Monkeys, 35 Dogs Lamented by UT Veterinary Official." *Houston Chronicle*, June 15, 2001.

Berkner, Alice B. *The Genesis of IBRRC*. IBRRC: International Bird Rescue Research Center. http://www.ibrrc.org/f_perspective.html.

———. "Wildlife Rehabilitation Techniques: Past, Present, and Future." Pp. 127–133 in *Proceedings of the 1979 U.S. Fish and Wildlife Service Pollution Response Workshop, 8–10 May, 1979, St. Petersburg, Florida*. Environmental Contaminant Evaluation Program. Washington, DC: U.S. Government Printing Office, 1979.

Best Friends Animal Society. *Not Left Behind: Rescuing the Pets of New Orleans*. New York: Yorkville Press, 2006.

Birke, Lynda. *Feminism, Animals, and Science*. Buckingham, UK: Open University Press, 1994.

———. "Who—or What—Are the Rats (and Mice) in the Laboratory?" *Society and Animals* 3 (2003): 207–224.

Birke, Lynda, Arnold Arluke, and Mike Michael. *The Sacrifice: How Scientific Experiments Transform Animals and People*. West Lafayette, IN: Purdue University Press, 2007.

Birkland, Thomas A. "In the Wake of the *Exxon Valdez*: How Environmental Disasters Can Spur Policy Change." *Environment* 40 (1998): 4–9, 27–32.

Blaikie, Piers, Terry Cannon, Ian Davis, and Ben Wisner. *At Risk: Natural Hazards, People's Vulnerability, and Disasters*. London: Routledge, 1994.

Bodkin, Jim, and Fred Weltz. "Evaluation of Sea Otter Capture after the T/V *Exxon Valdez* Oil Spill, Prince William Sound, Alaska." Pp. 61–69 in *Sea Otter Symposium: Proceedings of a Symposium to Evaluate the Response Effort on Behalf of Sea Otters after the T/V Exxon Valdez Oil Spill into Prince William Sound, Anchorage, Alaska*. U.S. Fish and Wildlife Service Biological Report 90. Washington DC: U.S. Government Printing Office, 1990.

Boersma, P. D. "Penguins Oiled in Argentina." *Science* 236 (1987): 135.

Bolin, Robert, and Lois Stanford. *The Northridge Earthquake: Vulnerability and Disaster*. London: Routledge, 1998.

Bourne, Joel K., Jr. "Gone with the Water." *National Geographic*, October 2004, 88–105.

Bowler, Ian R. "The Industrialization of Agriculture." Pp. 7–19 in *The Geography of Agriculture in Developed Market Economies*, edited by Ian R. Bowler. Essex, UK: Addison-Wesley Longman, 1992.

Brown, Darla. 2004. "A New Space, a New Day for the Animal Care Center." *UT-Houston Medicine Magazine*, Fall 2004, 14–15.

Bryndza, H. E., J. P. Foster Jr., J. H. McCartney, and J. C. Lober. "Methodology for Determining Surfactant Efficacy in Removal of Petrochemicals from Feathers." Pp. 69–86 in *Wildlife and Oil Spills: Response, Research, and Contingency Planning*, edited by L. Frink, K. Ball-Weir, and C. Smith. Hanover, PA: Sheridan Press, 1995.

Bukro, Casey. "U.S. Bureaucracy Halts Rescuers of Sea Otters." *Chicago Tribune*, April 9, 1989.

Burghardt, Gordon M., and Harold A. Herzog Jr. "Beyond Conspecifics: Is Brer Rabbit Our Brother?" *BioScience* 30 (1980): 763–768.

Carbone, Larry. *What Animals Want: Expertise and Advocacy in Laboratory Animal Welfare Policy*. New York: Oxford University Press, 2004.

Carter, Henry. "Oil and California's Seabirds: An Overview." *Marine Ornithology* 31 (2003): 1–7.

Cartmill, Matt. "Hunting and Humanity in Western Thought." *Social Research* 62 (1995): 773–786.

Cerulo, Karen. *Never Saw It Coming: Cultural Challenges to Envisioning the Worst.* Chicago: University of Chicago Press, 2006.

Clarke, K. C., and Jeffrey J. Hemphill. "The Santa Barbara Oil Spill: A Retrospective." Pp. 157–162 in *Yearbook of the Association of Pacific Coast Geographers*, vol. 64, edited by Darrick Danta. Honolulu: University of Hawai'i Press, 2002.

Cody, Cristal. "Tyson Shifting Its Ports on Gulf." *Arkansas Democrat-Gazette*, September 8, 2005.

Commission on the European Communities. *Communication from the Commission to the European Parliament and the Council on the Safety of the Seaborne Oil Trade.* Brussels: Commission on the European Communities, 2000.

Convery, Ian, Kathy Bailey, Maggie Mort, and Josephine Baxter. "Death in the Wrong Place: Emotional Geographies of the UK 2001 Foot and Mouth Disease Epidemic." *Journal of Rural Studies* 21 (2005): 99–109.

Cowan, Edward. *Oil and Water: The "Torrey Canyon" Disaster.* Philadelphia: Lippincott, 1968.

Crisp, Terri. *Emergency Animal Rescue Stories: True Stories about People Dedicated to Saving Animals from Disasters.* Roseville, CA: Prima, 2002.

Crisp, Terri, and Samantha Glen. *Out of Harm's Way: The Extraordinary True Story of One Woman's Lifelong Devotion to Animal Rescue.* New York: Pocket Books, 1997.

Crosby, F., S. Bromley, and L. Saxe. "Recent Unobtrusive Studies of Black and White Discrimination and Prejudice: A Literature Review." *Psychological Bulletin* 87 (1980): 546–563.

Cutter, S. L. *American Hazardscapes: The Regionalization of Hazards and Disasters.* Washington, DC: Joseph Henry Press, 2005.

Dahlheim, Marilyn E., and Craig O. Matkin. "Assessment of Injuries to Prince William Sound Orcas." Pp. 163–171 in *Marine Mammals and the Exxon Valdez*, edited by Thomas R. Loughlin. San Diego: Academic Press, 1994.

Dauphin, Gloria. *There's Something about Lily.* Louisiana SPCA, December 2005. http://www.la-spca.org/adoptions/tails/lily.htm.

Dawkins, Marian Stamp. "A User's Guide to Animal Welfare Science." *Trends in Ecology and Evolution* 21 (2005): 77–82.

DeGrazia, David. "The Ethics of Animal Research: What Are the Prospects for Agreement?" *Cambridge Quarterly of Healthcare Ethics* 8 (1999): 23–34.

Douglas, Mary. *How Institutions Think.* Syracuse NY: Syracuse University Press, 1986.

Dynes, Russell R. "The Disaster Event and Community Stress." Pp. 50–82 in *Organized Behavior in Disaster*, edited by Russell R. Dynes. Lexington, MA: Heath Lexington Books, 1970.

Erasmus, R. W., R. M. Randall, and B. M. Randall. "Oil Pollution, Insulation, and Body Temperatures in the Jackass Penguin (*Spheniscus demersus*)." *Comparative Biochemistry and Physiology* 69a (1981): 169–171.

Ernst, R. A. *University of California Cooperative Extension, Poultry Fact Sheet No. 20*. June 1995. animalscience.ucdavis.edu/Avian/pfs20.htm.

Estes, James A. "Catastrophes and Conservation: Lessons from Sea Otters and the Exxon Valdez." *Science* 254 (1991): 1596.

Fischetti, Mark. "Drowning New Orleans." *Scientific American*, October 2001, 76–85.

Foster, Mary. *Superdome Evacuations Enter Second Day*. Associated Press, September 1, 2005. http://www.breitbart.com/article.php?id=D8CBPBCG0&show_article=1.

Fothergill, Alice. "Gender, Risk, and Disaster." *International Journal of Mass Emergencies and Disasters* 14 (1996): 33–55.

Francione, Gary L. *Introduction to Animal Rights: Your Child or the Dog?* Philadelphia: Temple University Press, 2000.

Franklin, Adrian. *Animals and Modern Cultures: A Sociology of Human-Animal Relations in Modernity*. London: Sage, 1999.

Fry, D. M. "How Do You Fix the Loss of Half a Million Birds?" Pp. 30–33 in *Exxon Valdez Oil Spill Symposium, Program and Abstracts*. Anchorage: Exxon Valdez Oil Spill Trustee Council, 1993.

Fujimora, Joan. *Crafting Science: A Sociohistory of the Quest for the Genetics of Cancer*. Cambridge, MA: Harvard University Press, 1996.

Fulton, Jim. "Big Oil Plays a Dirty Game." *Toronto Globe and Mail*, July 20, 2000.

Gandini, P., P. D. Boersma, E. Frere, M. Gandini, T. Holik, and V. Lichtenstein. "Magellanic Penguins Affected by Chronic Petroleum Pollution along the Coast of Chubut, Argentina." *Auk* 111 (1994): 20–27.

García-Borboroglu, Pablo, P. Dee Boersma, Valeria Ruoppolo, Laura Reyes, Ginger A. Rebstock, Karen Griot, Sergio Rodrigues Heredia, Andrea Corrado Adornes, and Rodolfo Pinho da Silva. "Chronic Oil Pollution Harms Magellanic Penguins in the Southwest Atlantic." *Marine Pollution Bulletin* 52 (2006): 193–198.

Ginsberg, Thomas. 2005. "Lab Mice Meet Untimely Demise." *Philadelphia Inquirer*, August 5, 2005.

Glatz, Philip, Kim Critchley, and Kristine Lunam. "The Domestic Chicken." *ANZCCART News* (Glen Osmond SA, Australia) 9, no. 2 (June 1996). http://www.adelaide.edu.au/ANZCCART/publications/dom_chicken.pdf.

Gluck, John P., and Steven R. Kubacki. "Animals in Biomedical Research: The Undermining Effect of the Rhetoric of the Besieged." *Ethics and Behavior* 1 (1991): 157–173.

Goodwin, Brad. *Water, Water: Everywhere.* LAMA [Laboratory Animal Management Association] Disaster Preparedness Resource. http://www.lama-online.org/Brad1.html.

Gould, Steven Jay. *Wonderful Life: The Burgess Shale and the Nature of History.* New York: Norton, 1989.

Greek, C. Ray, and Jean Swingle Greek. *Sacred Cows and Golden Geese: The Human Costs of Experiments on Animals.* New York: Continuum, 2003.

Groves, Julian McAllister. *Hearts and Minds: The Controversy over Laboratory Animals.* Philadelphia: Temple University Press, 1996.

Gurian-Sherman, Doug. *CAFOs Uncovered: The Untold Cost of Confined Animal Feeding Operations.* Cambridge, MA: Union of Concerned Scientists, 2008. http://www.ucsusa.org/assets/documents/food_and_environment/CAFOs-Uncovered.pdf.

Gwynn, S. "The Case for Certain Cruelties." *Spectator* 123 (1924): 912–913.

Hackam, Daniel G., and Donald A. Redelmeier. "Translation of Research Evidence from Animals to Humans." *Journal of the American Medical Association* 296 (2006): 1731–1732.

Hall, Lee. *Capers in the Churchyard: Animal Rights Advocacy in the Age of Terror.* Darien, CT: Nectar Bat Press, 2006.

Hayes, Jennifer. *Sad and Emotional Day: Many Hurricane Ike Evacuees Chose to Leave without Their Pets.* Best Friends Network, September 18, 2005. http://network.bestfriends.org/rapidresponse/news/28980.html.

Haygood, Wil, and Ann Scot Tyson. "It Was as if All of Us Were Already Pronounced Dead." *Washington Post,* September 15, 2005.

Heath, Sebastian. *Animal Management in Disasters.* San Francisco: C. V. Mosby, 1999.

Heath, Sebastian, A. M. Beck, P. H. Kass, and L. T. Glickman. "Human and Pet Related Risk Factors for Household Evacuation Failure during a Natural Disaster." *American Journal of Epidemiology* 153 (2001): 659–665.

———. "Risk Factors for Pet Evacuation Failure after a Slow-Onset Disaster." *Journal of the American Veterinary Medical Association* 218 (2001): 1905–1910.

Heath, Sebastian, and Max Champion. "Human Health Concerns from Pet Ownership After a Tornado." *Prehospital and Disaster Medicine* 11 (1996): 67–70.

Heath, Sebastian, P. Kass, L. Hart, and G. Zompolis. "Epidemiological Study of Cats and Dogs Affected by the 1991 Oakland Fire." *Journal of the American Veterinary Medical Association* 212 (1998): 504–511.

Heath, Sebastian, and Andrea O'Shea. *Rescuing Rover: A First Aid and Disaster Guide for Dog Owners.* West Lafayette, IN: Purdue University Press, 1999.

Heath, Sebastian, S. K. Voeks, and L. T. Glickman. "Epidemiological Features of Pet Evacuation Failure in a Rapid-Onset Disaster." *Journal of the American Veterinary Medical Association* 218 (2001): 1898–1904.

Heredia, Sergio Rodríguez, Julio Loureiro, Karina Alvarez, Rosana Mattiello, and Valeria Ruoppolo. "Evolution of Penguin Rehabilitation at Fundación Mundo Marino, Argentina (1987–2006)." Pp. 49–54 in *Proceedings of the Ninth International Effects of Oil on Wildlife Conference,* edited by J. G. Massey. Davis: University of California Davis Wildlife Health Center, 2007.

Herzog, Harold A., Jr. "Conflicts of Interest: Kittens and Boa Constrictors, Pets and Research." *American Psychologist* 46 (1991): 246–247.

———. "Human Morality and Animal Research: Confessions and Quandaries." *American Scholar* 62 (1993): 337–349.

———. "The Moral Status of Mice." *American Psychologist* 43 (1988): 473–474.

Herzog, Harold A., Jr., Andrew Rowan, and Daniel Kossow. "Social Attitudes to Animals." Pp. 55–69 in *The State of Animals: 2001,* edited by D. J. Salem and A. N. Rowan. Washington, DC: Humane Society Press, 2001.

Heubeck, Martin, Kees C. J. Camphuysen, Roberto Bao, Diana Humple, Antoniao Sandoval Rey, Bernard Cadiou, Stefan Bräger, and Tim Thomas. "Assessing the Impact of Major Oil Spills on Seabird Populations." *Marine Pollution Bulletin* 26 (2003): 900–902.

Hewitt, Kenneth, ed. *Interpretations of Calamity: From the Viewpoint of Human Ecology.* London: Allen and Unwin, 1983.

———. *Regions of Risk: A Geographical Introduction to Disasters.* London: Longman, 1997.

Holstein, James A., and Gale Miller, eds. *Reconsidering Social Constructionism: Debates in Social Problems Theory.* New York: Aldine de Gruyter, 1993.

Humane Research Council. *Advocating Meat Reduction and Vegetarianism to Adults in the U.S.* Seattle: Humane Research Council, 2007.

Ibrahim, Darian M. *Reduce, Refine, Replace: The Failure of the Three R's and the Future of Animal Experimentation.* University of Chicago Legal Forum, 2006; Arizona Legal Studies Discussion Paper no. 06-17. Available at http://ssrn.com/abstract=888206.

Institute for Laboratory Animal Research, Commission on Life Sciences, National Research Council. *Guide for the Care and Use of Laboratory Animals.* Washington, DC: National Academies Press, 1996.

International Bird Rescue Research Center (IBRRC). "Founder Alice Berkner Reflects on IBRRC's History." *On the Wing,* Spring 2007, 4. http://www.ibrrc.org/pdfs/OnTheWing_Spring_07_web.pdf.

————. *New Year, New Hope: Spain Prepares for Long "Prestige" Oil Spill Clean-Up; More Birds to Be Released.* January 8, 2003. http://www.ibrrc.org/spain_spill_response.html.

————. "35 Years of Advancing Aquatic Bird Rehabilitation and Research." *On the Wing,* Spring 2007, 6. http://www.ibrrc.org/pdfs/OnTheWing_Spring_07_web.pdf.

————. *20,000 Patient Penguins: Responding to the World's Largest Seabird Rehabilitation Effort in South Africa.* http://www.ibrrc.org/treasure_report_1.html.

International Petroleum Industry Environmental Conservation Association (IPIECA). *A Guide to Oiled Wildlife Response Planning.* IPIECA Report Series, vol. 13. London: IPIECA, 2004.

International Working Group on Animals in Disasters. *Protecting Animals from Disasters.* London: World Society for the Protection of Animals, 2007.

Irons, David B., Timothy D. Bowman, Wallace P. Erickson, Lyman L. McDonald, and Bryan K. Lance. "Nine Years after the Exxon Valdez Oil Spill: Effects on Marine Bird Populations in Prince William Sound, Alaska." *Condor* 102 (2000): 723–737.

Irvine, Leslie. "Animals in Disasters: Issues for Animal Liberation Activism and Policy." *Journal for Critical Animal Studies* 4 (2006): 1–16. http://www.cala-online.org/Journal/Journal_Articles_download/Issue_5/irvine.pdf.

————. *Animals in Disasters: Responsibility and Action.* Ann Arbor, MI: Animals and Society Institute, 2007.

————. *If You Tame Me: Understanding Our Connection with Animals.* Philadelphia: Temple University Press, 2004.

————. "The Problem of Unwanted Pets: A Case Study in How Institutions 'Think' about Clients' Needs." *Social Problems* 50 (2003): 550–566.

————. *Providing for Pets during Disasters: An Exploratory Study.* Quick Response Research Report 171, Natural Hazards Research Center, University of Colorado, 2004. http://www.colorado.edu/hazards/research/qr/qr171/qr171.html.

————. *Providing for Pets during Disasters, Part II: Animal Response Volunteers in Gonzalez, Louisiana.* Quick Response Research Report 187, Natural Hazards Research Center, University of Colorado, 2006. http://www.colorado.edu/hazards/research/qr/qr187/qr187.html.

Jamieson, Dale. "Against Zoos." Pp. 108–117 in *In Defense of Animals,* edited by Peter Singer. New York: Basil Blackwell, 1985.

Jehl, R. J. "Mortality of Magellanic Penguins in Argentina." *Auk* 92 (1975): 596–598.

Jones, Don, Glenn Carpenter, Karl VanDevender, and Peter Wright. *Fact Sheet #13B: CAFO Requirements for Large Swine Operations.* Livestock and Poultry Environmental Stewardship Curriculum, Iowa State University, 2003. http://www.lpes.org/cafo/13bFS_Swine.pdf.

Jones, Leigh. "TV Show Features Ike Pet." *Galveston County Daily News*, January 1, 2009.

Kalof, Linda. *Looking at Animals in Human History*. London: Reaktion, 2007.

Kannan, G., and Joy A. Mench. "Influence of Different Handling Methods and Crating Periods on Plasma Corticosterone Concentrations in Broilers." *British Poultry Science* 37 (1996): 21–31.

Kieswer, Kristine. "PCRM Urges Texas Medical Center Not to Replace Animals Killed in Flood." *Good Medicine* X (Autumn 2001). http://www.pcrm.org/magazine/GM01Autumn/GM01Autumn.html.

Kinney, Aaron. "'Looting' or 'Finding'? Bloggers Are Outraged over the Different Captions on Photos of Blacks and Whites in New Orleans." *Salon.com*, September 1, 2005. http://dir.salon.com/story/news/feature/2005/09/01/photo_controversy/index.html.

Kirby, Alex. "Spanish Spill Not Over Yet." *Alexander's Gas and Oil Connections*, November 22, 2003. http://www.gasandoil.com/goc/news/nte34856.htm.

Klinenberg, Eric. *Heat Wave: A Social Autopsy of Disaster in Chicago*. Chicago: University of Chicago Press, 2002.

Knabb, Richard D., Jamie R. Rhome, and Daniel P. Brown, *Tropical Cyclone Report: Hurricane Katrina, 23–30 August 2005*. Washington, DC: National Hurricane Center, December 20, 2005; updated August 10, 2006. http://www.nhc.noaa.gov/pdf/TCR-AL122005_Katrina.pdf.

Knorr-Cetina, Karin. *Epistemic Cultures: How the Sciences Make Knowledge*. Cambridge, MA: Harvard University Press, 1999.

La Follette, Hugh, and Niall Shanks. *Brute Science: Dilemmas of Animal Experimentation*. London: Routledge, 1994.

Latour, Bruno, and Steven Woolgar. *Laboratory Life: The Construction of Scientific Facts*. London: Sage, 1979.

Lawrence, Elizabeth. "Neoteny in American Perceptions of Animals." *Journal of Psychoanalytic Anthropology* 9 (1986): 41–54.

Leben, Robert, George Born, and Jim Scott. *CU-Boulder Researchers Chart Katrina's Growth in Gulf of Mexico*. University of Colorado at Boulder press release, September 15, 2005. http://www.colorado.edu/news/releases/2005/358.html.

Leslie, Jeff, and Cass R. Sunstein. "Animal Rights without Controversy." *Law and Contemporary Problems* 70 (2007): 117–138.

Lim, Grace. "Research Monkeys Fall Victim to False AIDS Rumor." *Miami Herald*, September 6, 1992.

Linnabary, R. D., and John C. New Jr. "Results of a Survey of Emergency Evacuation of Dairy Cattle." *Journal of the American Veterinary Medical Association* 202 (1993): 1238–1242.

Linnabary, R. D., John C. New Jr., R. F. Hall, and E. H. Usrey. "Attitudinal Survey of Tennessee Beef Producers Regarding Evacuation during Emergency." *Journal of the American Veterinary Medical Association* 199 (1991): 1022–1026.

Lobao, Linda, and Katherine Meyer. "The Great Agricultural Transition: Crisis, Change, and Social Consequences of Twentieth Century U.S. Farming." *Annual Review of Sociology* 27 (2001): 103–124.

Logan, Cheryl A. "Before There Were Standards: The Role of Test Animals in the Production of Empirical Generality in Physiology." *Journal of the History of Biology* 35 (2002): 329–363.

Loseke, Donileen R. *Thinking about Social Problems: An Introduction to Constructionist Perspectives.* New York: Aldine de Gruyter, 1999.

Lynch, Michael E. "Sacrifice and the Transformation of the Animal Body into a Scientific Object: Laboratory Culture and Ritual Practice in the Neurosciences." *Social Studies of Science* 18 (1988): 265–289.

Maher, Brendan A. "Test Tubes with Tails: How Mice Help Play out Science's Best Laid Plans." *Scientist* 16 (2002): 22.

Mallin, Michael A., and Catherine A. Corbett. "How Hurricane Attributes Determine the Extent of Environmental Effects: Multiple Hurricanes and Different Coastal Systems." *Estuaries and Coasts* 29 (2006): 1046–1061.

Mallin, Michael A., M. H. Posey, M. R. McIver, D. C. Parsons, S. H. Ensign, and T. D. Alphin. "Impacts and Recovery from Multiple Hurricanes in a Piedmont-Coastal Plain River System." *BioScience* 52 (2002): 999–1010.

McCrary, Michael D., David O. Panzer, and Mark O. Pierson. "Oil and Gas Operations Offshore California: Status, Risks, and Safety." *Marine Ornithology* 31 (2003): 43–49.

McKinlay, John B., and Sonja McKinlay. "The Questionable Contribution of Medical Measures to the Decline of Mortality in the United States in the Twentieth Century." *Health and Society* 55 (1977): 405–428.

McKinlay, John B., Sonja McKinlay, and Robert Beaglehole. "A Review of the Evidence concerning the Impact of Medical Measures on Recent Mortality and Morbidity in the United States." *International Journal of Health Services* 19 (1989): 81–208.

McLaughlin, Mike. *Center Says State Must Act to Prevent Hurricane Damage.* North Carolina Center for Public Policy Research press release, December 11, 2001. http://www.nccppr.org/easternnc1.htm.

McQuaid, John, and Mark Schleifstein. "In Harm's Way." *Times-Picayune*, June 23, 2002.

———. "Left Behind." *Times-Picayune*, June 24, 2002.

Mead, Chris. "Cleaned but Not Saved?" *Bird On! News*, May 15, 1996. http://www.birdcare.com/bin/shownews/22.

———. "Poor Prospects for Oiled Birds." *Nature* 390 (1997): 449–450.

Mearns, Alan J. "*Exxon Valdez* Shoreline Treatment and Operations: Implications for Response, Assessment, Monitoring, and Research." Pp. 309–328 in *Proceedings of the Exxon Valdez Oil Spill Symposium Held at Anchorage, Alaska, USA, 2–5 February 1993*, edited by S. D. Rice, R. B. Spies, D. A. Wolfe, and B. A. Wright. Bethesda, MD: American Fisheries Society, 1996.

Miller, E. A., and S. C. Welte. "Caring for Oiled Birds." Pp. 301–309 in *Zoo and Wild Animal Medicine, Current Therapy 4*, edited by Murray E. Fowler and R. Eric Miller. Philadelphia: W. B. Saunders, 1999.

Miller, Gale, and James A. Holstein. "On the Sociology of Social Problems." Pp. 1–16 in *Perspectives on Social Problems*, vol. 1, edited by J. Holstein and G. Miller. Greenwich, CT: JAI Press, 1989.

Molnar, Joseph, Thomas Hoban, and Gail Bryant. "Passing the Cluck, Dodging Pullets: Corporate Power, Environmental Responsibility, and the Contract Poultry Grower." *Southern Rural Sociology* 18 (2002): 88–110.

Mort, Maggie, Ian Convery, Josephine Baxter, and Cathy Bailey. "Animal Disease and Human Trauma: The Psychosocial Implications of the 2001 UK Foot and Mouth Disease Disaster." *Journal of Applied Animal Welfare Science* 11 (2008): 133–148.

National Oceanic and Atmospheric Administration. Hazardous Materials Assessment and Response Division. *Oil Spill Case Histories 1967–1991: Summaries of Significant U.S. and International Spills.* Report #HMRAD 92-11. Seattle: NOAA/Hazardous Materials Assessment and Response Division, 1992.

National Research Council. *Guide for the Care and Use of Laboratory Animals.* Washington, DC: National Academies Press, 1996.

———. *Oil in the Sea III: Inputs, Fates, and Effects.* Washington, DC: National Academies Press, 2003.

Nerlich, Brigitte, Sam Hillyard, and Nick Wright. "Stress and Stereotypes: Children's Reactions to the Outbreak of Foot and Mouth Disease in the UK in 2001." *Children and Society* 19 (2005): 348–359.

Newman, Scott H., Mike H. Ziccardi, Alice B. Berkner, Jay Holcomb, Curt Clumpner, and Jonna A. K. Mazet. "A Historical Account of Oiled Wildlife Care in California." *Marine Ornithology* 31 (2003): 59–64.

Norwood, F. Bailey, Jayson L. Lusk, and Robert W. Prickett. *Consumer Preferences for Farm Animal Welfare: Results of a Nationwide Telephone Survey.* Working paper, Department of Agricultural Economics, Oklahoma State University, 2007. http://asp.okstate.edu/baileynorwood/AW2/InitialReporttoAFB.pdf.

Olsen, Lise. "City Had Evacuation Plan but Strayed from Strategy." *Houston Chronicle*, September 8, 2005. http://www.chron.com/disp/story.mpl/nation/3344347.html.

Orlans, F. Barbara. "Data on Animal Experimentation in the United States: What They Do and Do Not Show." *Perspectives in Biology and Medicine* 37 (1994): 217–231.

———. "The Injustice of Excluding Laboratory Rats, Mice, and Birds from the Animal Welfare Act." *Kennedy Institute of Ethics Journal* 10 (2000): 229–238.

Orlans, F. Barbara, Tom Beauchamp, Rebecca Dresser, David B. Morton, and John P. Gluck. *The Human Use of Animals: Case Studies in Ethical Choice.* New York: Oxford University Press, 1998.

Ott, Riki. *Sound Truths and Corporate Myth$: The Legacy of the Exxon Valdez Oil Spill.* Cordova, AK: Dragonfly Sisters Press, 2005.

Park, Miyun. "The Lucky Few." *Satya,* November 2005. http://www.satyamag.com/nov05/park.html.

Patterson, James T. *The Dread Disease: Cancer and Modern American Culture.* Cambridge, MA: Harvard University Press, 1987.

Peacock, Walter Gillis, Betty Hearn Morrow, and Hugh Gladwin, eds. *Hurricane Andrew: Ethnicity, Gender, and the Sociology of Disasters.* New York: Routledge, 1997.

Peny, R. W., M. K. Lindell, and M. R. Greene. "Evacuation Experiences and the Evacuation Planning Process." Pp. 121–150 in *Evacuation Planning in Emergency Management,* edited by R. W. Peny, M. K. Lindell, and M. R. Greene. Lexington, MA: Lexington Books, 1981.

Perel, Pablo, Ian Roberts, Emily Sena, Philipa Wheble, Catherine Briscoe, Peter Sandercock, Malcolm Macleod, Luciano E. Mignini, Pradeep Jayaram, and Khalid S Khan. "Comparison of Treatment Effects between Animal Experiments and Clinical Trials: Systematic Review." *British Medical Journal* 334 (2007): 197.

Perrow, Charles. *The Next Catastrophe: Reducing Our Vulnerabilities to Natural, Industrial, and Terrorist Disasters.* Princeton, NJ: Princeton University Press, 2007.

Pew Commission on Industrial Farm Animal Production. *Putting Meat on the Table: Industrial Farm Animal Production in America.* 2008. http://www.ncifap.org/_images/PCIFAPFin.pdf.

Phillips, Mary T. "Proper Names and the Social Construction of Biography: The Negative Case of Laboratory Animals." *Qualitative Sociology* 17 (1994): 119–143.

Phinizy, Coles. "The Lost Pets That Stray to the Lab." *Sports Illustrated,* November 27, 1965, 36–49.

Piatt, J. F., and R. G. Ford. "How Many Seabirds Were Killed by the *Exxon Valdez* Oil Spill?" Pp. 712–719 in *Proceedings of the Exxon Valdez Oil Spill Symposium Held at Anchorage, Alaska, USA, 2–5 February 1993,* edited by

S. D. Rice, R. B. Spies, D. A. Wolfe, and B. A. Wright. Bethesda, MD: American Fisheries Society, 1996.

Piatt, J. F., and C. J. Lensink. "*Exxon Valdez* Bird Toll." *Nature* 342 (1989): 865–866.

Piatt, J. F., C. J. Lensink, W. Butler, M. Kendziorek, and D. R. Nysewander. "Immediate Impact of the 'Exxon Valdez' Oil Spill on Marine Birds." *Auk* 107 (1990): 387–397.

Plous, Scott. "Attitudes toward the Use of Animals in Psychological Research and Education: Results from a National Survey of Psychologists. *American Psychologist* 51 (1996): 1167–1180.

———. "Psychological Mechanisms in the Human Use of Animals." *Journal of Social Issues* 49 (1993): 11–52.

Plous, Scott, and Harold A. Herzog Jr. "Poll Shows Researchers Favor Lab Animal Protection." *Science* 290 (2000): 711.

———. "Should the Animal Welfare Act Cover Rats, Mice, and Birds? The Results of an IACUC Survey." *Lab Animal* 38 (1999): 40.

Potter, Jeffrey. *Disaster by Oil.* New York: Macmillan, 1973.

Pound, Pandora, Shah Ebrahim, Peter Sandercock, Michael B. Bracken, and Ian Roberts. "Where Is the Evidence That Animal Research Benefits Humans?" *British Medical Journal* 328 (2004): 514–517.

Rader, Karen A. *Making Mice: Standardizing Animals for American Biomedical Research 1900–1955.* Princeton, NJ: Princeton University Press, 2004.

———. "'The Mouse People': Murine Genetics at the Bussey Institution, 1909–1936." *Journal of the History of Biology* 31 (1998): 327–354.

———. "The Multiple Meanings of Laboratory Animals: Standardizing Mice for American Cancer Research, 1910–1950." Pp. 389–438 in *Animals in Human Histories*, edited by M. Henniger-Voss. Rochester, NY: University of Rochester Press, 2002.

Ramirez, Michael. "'My Dog's Just Like Me': Dog Ownership as a Gender Display." *Symbolic Interaction* 29 (2006): 373–391.

Ramseur, Jonathan L. *Oil Spills in U.S. Coastal Waters: Background, Governance, and Issues for Congress.* Washington, DC: Congressional Research Service, Library of Congress, 2007. http://www.ncseonline.org/NLE/CRSreports/07May/RL33705.pdf.

Regan, Tom. *The Case for Animal Rights.* Berkeley: University of California Press, 1987.

Reid, Stafford, Chris Battaglia, and Coleen Doucette. "A Review of Factors That Influence Reasonable Cost and Actions within Oiled Wildlife Response." Pp. 146–155 in *Proceedings of the Ninth International Effects of Oil on Wildlife Conference*, edited by J. G. Massey. Davis: University of California Davis Wildlife Health Center, 2007.

Ridoux, Vincent, Lionel Lafontaine, Paco Bustamante, Florence Caurant, Willy Dabin, Cécile Delcroix, Sami Hassani, et al. "The Impact of the 'Erika' Oil Spill on Pelagic and Coastal Marine Mammals: Combining Demographic, Ecological, Trace Metals and Biomarker Evidences." *Aquatic Living Resources* 17 (2004): 379–387.

Risk Management Solutions. *Tropical Storm Allison, June 2001.* RMS Event Report. Newark, CA: Risk Management Solutions, 2001.

Ritvo, Harriet. *The Animal Estate: The English and Other Creatures in the Victorian Age.* Cambridge, MA: Harvard University Press, 1987.

Roberts, Ian, Irene Kwan, Phillip Evans, and Steven Haig. "Does Animal Experimentation Inform Human Healthcare? Observations from a Systematic Review of International Animal Experiments on Fluid Resuscitation." *British Medical Journal* 324 (2002): 474–476.

Rodríguez, Havidán, and John Barnshaw. "The Social Construction of Disasters: From Heat Waves to Worst-Case Scenarios." *Contemporary Sociology* 35 (2006): 218–223.

Rollin, Bernard E. *The Unheeded Cry: Animal Consciousness, Animal Pain, and Sentience.* Oxford: Oxford University Press, 1980.

Ronconi, Robert A., Colleen Cassady St. Clair, Patrick D. O'Hara, and Alan E. Burger. "Waterbird Deterrence at Oil Spills and Other Hazardous Sites: Potential Applications of a Radar-Activated On-Demand Deterrence System." *Marine Ornithology* 32 (2004): 25–33.

Rudacille, Deborah. *The Scalpel and the Butterfly: The Conflict between Animal Research and Animal Protection.* New York: Farrar, Straus and Giroux, 2000.

Ruoppolo, Valeria, P. Dee Boersma, Pablo Garcia Borboroglu, Laura M. Reyes, and Rodolfo Pinho da Silva. *Chronic Oiling Affecting Magellanic Penguins: A Review.* 2003. http://www.ibrrc.org/pdfs/EOW03_Chronic_oiling.pdf.

Ruoppolo, Valeria, Barbara Callahan, Rodolofo P. Silva Filhol, Sergio R. Heredia, Karen Griot, Ricardo Matus, and Jay Holcomb. "Update on the IFAW Penguin Network: Presenting Goals and Achievements since 2001." Pp. 156–160 in *Proceedings of the Ninth International Effects of Oil on Wildlife Conference*, edited by J. G. Massey. Davis: University of California Davis Wildlife Health Center, 2007.

Russell, William S., and Rex L. Burch. *The Principles of Humane Experimental Technique.* London: Methuen, 1959.

Ryder, Richard D. *Victims of Science: The Use of Animals in Research.* London: Davis-Poynter, 1975.

Salman, M. D., John G. New, Janet M. Scarlett, Philip H. Kass, Rebecca Ruch-Gallie, and Suzanne Hetts. "Human and Animal Factors Related to the Relinquishment of Dogs and Cats to Twelve Selected Animal Shelters in the United States." *Journal of Applied Animal Welfare Science* 1 (1998): 207–226.

Sambidi, Pramod R., Wes Harrison, and A. J. Farr. *A Conjoint Analysis of Site Selection for the U.S. Broiler Industry: Implications for Louisiana.* Baton Rouge: Louisiana State University Agricultural Center, 2004.

Schub, Tanja. "The Year of the Flood: Tropical Storm Allison's Impact on the Texas Medical Center." *Lab Animal* 31 (2002): 34–39.

Scott, Cathy. *Update on Saint Bernard Parish Murders.* February 24, 2006. http://noanimalleftbehind.blogspot.com/2006_02_19_archive.html.

Scully, Matthew. *Dominion: The Power of Man, the Suffering of Animals, and the Call to Mercy.* New York: St. Martin's, 2002.

Sen, Amartya. *Poverty and Famine: An Essay on Entitlement and Deprivation.* Oxford: Oxford University Press, 1982.

Serpell, James. *In the Company of Animals.* 1986. Reprint, Oxford: Basil Blackwell, 1996.

Shapiro, Kenneth. "A Rodent for Your Thoughts: The Social Construction of Animal Models." Pp. 439–469 in *Animals in Human Histories,* edited by M. Henniger-Voss. Rochester, NY: University of Rochester Press, 2002.

Sharp, Brian. "Post Release Survival of Oiled, Cleaned Seabirds in North America." *Ibis* 138 (1996): 222–228.

Sharp, Lynn. "Chasing Birds from Oil Spills: Two Experiments." *Coastal Zone* 7 (1987): 1–15.

Sigma Xi. "Sigma Xi Statement of the Use of Animals in Research." *American Scientist* 80 (1992): 73–86.

Singer, Peter. *Animal Liberation: A New Ethics for Our Treatment of Animals.* New York: Avon Books, 1975.

Smith, Richard. "Comroe and Dripps Revisited." *British Medical Journal* 295 (1987): 1404–1407.

Specter, Michael. "Lab Mishap Destroys AIDS Mice; NIH Worker Cut Off Air by Accident." *Washington Post,* December 8, 1988.

Staats, Joan. "The Laboratory Mouse." Pp. 1–9 in *Biology of the Laboratory Mouse,* edited by E. L. Green. 2nd ed. New York: McGraw Hill, 1966.

Starmer, Elanor, and Timothy A. Wise. *Feeding at the Trough: Industrial Livestock Firms Saved $35 Billion from Low Feed Prices.* GDAE Policy Brief 07-03. Medford, MA: Global Development and Environment Institute, Tufts University, December 2007. http://www.ase.tufts.edu/gdae/Pubs/rp/PB07-03FeedingAtTroughDec07.pdf.

Steinfeld, Henning, Pierre Gerber, Tom Wassenaar, Vincent Castel, Mauricio Rosales, and Cees de Haan. *Livestock's Long Shadow: Environmental Issues and Options.* Rome: Food and Agriculture Organization of the United Nations, 2006.

Stormont, Leana. "Help Was Never on the Way." *Satya*, November 2005. http://www.satyamag.com/nov05/stormont.html.

Tajfel, Henry, and A. L. Wilkes. "Classification and Quantitative Judgment." *British Journal of Psychology* 54 (1963): 101–114.

Tierney, Kathleen. "Foreshadowing Katrina: Recent Sociological Contributions to Vulnerability Science." *Contemporary Sociology* 35 (2006): 207–212.

Tippee, Bob. "The Prestige Spill Raises Questions of Accountability." *Oil and Gas Journal* 100 (2002): 68.

United Egg Producers. *United Egg Producers Animal Husbandry Guidelines for U.S. Egg Laying Flocks*. Alpharetta, GA.: United Egg Producers, 2005.

U.S. Department of Agriculture. Economic Research Service. *Poultry Yearbook 2004*, 2006. Available from http://usda.mannlib.cornell.edu/MannUsda/viewDocumentInfo.do?documentID=1367.

———. National Agricultural Statistics Service. *Livestock Slaughter: 2004 Annual Summary*, 2005. http://usda.mannlib.cornell.edu/reports/nassr/livestock/pls-bban/lsan0305.pdf.

———. National Agricultural Statistics Service. *Poultry Slaughter: 2004 Annual Summary*, 2005. http://usda.mannlib.cornell.edu/reports/nassr/poultry/ppy-bban/pslaan05.pdf.

Vaughan, Diane. *The Challenger Launch Decision: Risky Technology, Culture, and Deviance at NASA*. Chicago: University of Chicago Press, 1999.

Vince, Gaia. "Prestige Oil Spill Far Worse Than Thought." *NewScientist*, August 27, 2003. http://www.newscientist.com/article.ns?id=dn4100.

Von Sydow, Oscar. "Sizing Up the Bulk Sector." *Surveyor*, Winter 2002, 3–9.

Walsh, Diana. 2005. "1,000 Chickens That Rode Out the Storm Now Escape the Frying Pan." *San Francisco Chronicle*, September 13, 2005.

Wayman, Stan. "Concentration Camps for Lost and Stolen Pets." *LIFE*, February 4, 1996, 22–29.

Weaver, Warren, Jr. "Senate Hearing Held." *New York Times*, February 6, 1969.

West B., and B-X. Zhou. "Did Chickens Go North? New Evidence for Domestication." *World's Poultry Science Journal* 45 (1989): 205–218.

Whisson, Desley A., and John Y. Takekawa. *Testing the Effectiveness of an Aquatic Hazing Device on Waterbirds in San Francisco Bay, California*. Report to the California Department of Fish and Game, Oil Spill Prevention, and Response, University of California Davis. 1998. http://www.werc.usgs.gov/sfbe/pdfs/Whisson-Takekawa1998.pdf.

Wilder, D. A. "Social Categorization: Implications for Creation and Reduction of Intergroup Bias." Pp. 291–355 in *Advances in Experimental Social Psychology*, edited by L. Berkowitz. New York: Academic Press, 1986.

Wing, S., S. Freedman, and L. Band. "The Potential Impact of Flooding on Confined Animal Feeding Operations in Eastern North Carolina." *Environmental Health Perspectives* 110 (2002): 387–391.

Wise, Steven M. *Rattling the Cage: Toward Legal Rights for Animals.* Cambridge, MA: Perseus, 2000.

Wise, Timothy A. *Identifying the Real Winners from U.S. Agricultural Policies.* GDAE Working Paper no. 05-07. 2005. http://www.ase.tufts.edu/gdae/Pubs/wp/05-07RealWinnersUSAg.pdf.

Yergin, Daniel. *The Prize: The Epic Quest for Oil, Money, and Power.* New York: Simon & Schuster, 1991.

Index